Cabin Fever

Special Places in My Heart

George Naugle

Scotland
PRESS

CABIN FEVER
SPECIAL PLACES IN MY HEART

Scotland Press
3583 Scotland Road
Building 70
Scotland PA 17254

ISBN-13: 978-1-941746-42-4 (Hardcover)
ISBN-13: 978-1-941746-43-1 (Paperback)
ISBN-13: 978-1-941746-44-8 (E-book)

Cabin Fever

Special Places in My Heart

A chronicle of two hunting camps, some stories about events that happened in them, and perhaps an explanation of why I love both places so much.

Camp Rip-N-Tear: High on a hilltop in the Laurel Highlands of Pennsylvania

Dedication

This book is dedicated to the memory of a good friend who passed from this mortal coil in December of 2016, Richard "Rick" Steinmiller. Rick owned a hunting camp just half a mile from Camp Rip-N-Tear, our hunting cabin in Somerset County, Pennsylvania. Over the ten years I knew him, we became the kind of friends that sometimes get phone calls out of the blue to discuss life as it was and would be if we were put in charge. Rick was a former U. S. Marine, and we thank him for his service to our country. In later years, he did not hunt as hard, but he still loved the time spent in camp, as do I. RIP, Rick. Semper Fi.

Rick Steinmiller on a much better day in November, 2010.

Table of Contents

SECTION II : CAMP RIP-N-TEAR

Acknowledgements

This work did not turn out to be what I normally think of as a book. I decided that it had to be in print, though. The narrative spans thirty years, perhaps the best thirty years of my life, and those who contributed to it should be remembered.

A book such as this does not come into being without help, and lots of it. Once again, I must give credit to my wife of over 57 years. Ms. Doris served as my editor one more time. While I sometimes get frustrated with the pace of editing one of my manuscripts, I have to admit that the finished product is quantum leaps better in quality. I am cursed with the ability to read rather fast, and I write the same way. Doris takes my work and makes it worth reading. I should also mention my publishers of the Scotland Group, Dean Drawbaugh and David Newell. They did a lot that I can't do.

A number of hunting buddies grace the following pages. Fellow members of my first hunting camp, Camp Bucktail, included Donald "Pat" Haller, William H. "Bill" Lloyd, John Bartholow, and Charles "Beetle" Bailey. Some other people you will meet hunted as guests there. Bill Lloyd's brother Howard and his boys, Larry and Bill Dubbs, Nick Sabetto, Larry Guise, and David Hartman consumed some stew, climbed the hills, and contributed much to the enjoyment of camp. A couple of neighbors, Andrew Grissinger and his son Steve, became friends. We hunted together for over twenty years. When I made the move to Camp Rip-N-Tear, a cabin in southern Somerset County, Pennsylvania, Dave and Larry went along, as did Nick Sabetto, until he decided to give up hunting. My son-in-law, Crawford Peters, who is half-owner of the new camp also re-entered the picture. Dave's nephew, Judd showed up on occasion. Several of Crawford's friends and his son Seth hunted with us from time to time, and also helped out on various projects. A big thank you goes to all who have made my time in camp better than it would have been without you.

Introduction

Way back when I was only twelve years old, a neighbor, Theorus (Thor) Ebert, who had taken me under his wing, let me tag along to his hunting cabin in Potter County, Pennsylvania. I can't even remember the name of that cabin. It sat at the bottom of the mountain on the southern side of Windfall Hollow where Big Bench Trail began. There was a spring on the hillside for water and lots of firewood for a youngster to learn the technique of splitting it with an axe. I didn't kill anything other than a couple of squirrels on that trip, but something was kindled in my mind. I loved that cabin and later resolved that someday I would have one of my own.

Several years later, during the early 1960s, I visited that cabin one more time. Some older guys, one of them Ted Bear who had built the cabin, were there. I used the skills learned on that first trip and split a bunch of wood for their stove. It was sort of like a reunion, as Ted had taught the hunter safety course I attended at age twelve. During the following decades, I was convinced that my ultimate hunting camp had to be in the mountains of north central Pennsylvania.

For a number of years after graduating from high school, I made a trip to northern Pennsylvania to hunt deer and bears. For a while, a group of us including Bob Miller, a math teacher who taught across the hall from me, hunted the area around Sinnemahoning in Cameron County and a huge wild area including Wykoff Run and the Quehanna preserve. We usually took Bob's brother Tom Hoy and his buddy Hank Baker along. These were the first of a number of youngsters I have mentored. We would set up a tent camp near George Stevenson Dam and hunt the area. Bob Bitner and Paul DeWalt, two men I knew from my days growing up in New Cumberland, owned a cabin on the hillside above the dam. They had a second camp that was constructed from a trailer which they offered to sell us for $500. At that time, the price might as well have been a million dollars. I had barely a couple of bucks to my name, so we had to turn that offer down.

Bitner and DeWalt were two very interesting guys. Both had been snipers in World War II, and they loved long range shooting. Both shot at the Williamsport, Pennsylvania, 1000-yard shoot, and sometimes placed in it. Their method of hunting was to set up a shooting table and spotting scope on a ridge where they could overlook a facing ridge and scan it for deer. While we were there that first time, Bitner took a six-point buck at a distance of over 700 yards. Some shooting skill!

Time passed, over twenty years of it. Bob Miller and I moved our hunting for deer to Black Log Valley on the border between Juniata and Huntingdon Counties. By this time, another Shippensburg teacher, Pat Haller, had joined our group. Sometimes we camped overnight in the back of a pickup truck, but usually we just drove to the hunt early in the morning. This area was a whole lot closer to home, requiring only about an hour drive, and deer and turkeys were plentiful. We hunted that area for nearly two decades until the late 1980s. It was fairly easy hunting since we could drive into the hunting area on a dirt road. Not much climbing being necessary, we did not work up a sweat.

During deer season of 1985, a tract of land in Black Log Valley owned by a man who was related to our former guidance counselor, Buzz Clark, became available. A group of us, which at this time included myself, Pat Haller, Chuck Bailey, and Bill Lloyd, decided to buy it and build a cabin, but at the last minute, Mr. Clark withdrew his offer and sold the land to someone else. The dream was put on hold.

In 1986, my dream of having a hunting camp became a reality, as the stories following this will show. Three of us purchased a cabin on a tract of land located just north of the Huntingdon/Fulton County line, and this served as our base of operations for quite some time. Chuck Bailey decided not to join us because of his impending marriage. Bob Miller had decided in the meantime to limit his hunting to the South Mountain near Shippensburg. He and I drifted apart during the following years.

In 2007, my son-in-law and I came to own a camp in southern Somerset County. During the next few years, I moved my hunting there, and we continue to build memories. Dave Hartman and Larry Guise, who hunted with me as guests at the first camp, came along with the move.

A hunting camp is a home base for hunting. It ends up generating a whole lot of memories. Over time, it becomes a place in the heart for a hunter such as me who loves to hunt. Camps develop a personality of their own. Some are spartan, as was Camp Bucktail, having no running water and when we bought it, not even an outhouse. We purchased a "job johnny" to fill the need for that latter item. Some, like my second camp, Camp Rip-N-Tear, have lots of amenities, including electricity, plumbing, and air conditioning. Whatever the camp provides in the way of creature comforts pales in comparison to the experiences and memories it creates. What will follow is a chronicle of my experiences at two hunting camps, interspersed with a few stories I have written that seem to be appropriate in conveying this thinking. I hope the reader enjoys the stories, but there is no way he can enjoy them as much as I enjoyed doing the things that generated those stories. Some have been previously published in one or the other of my two "Luckiest Hunter" books. So, with that in mind, here we go.

Photo taken of Camp Bucktail during fall, 1987

SECTION I

Camp Bucktail

1986: A Camp Becomes A Reality

A group of teachers at Shippensburg High School, Bill Lloyd, Chuck Bailey, Pat Haller, and I, met to explore the idea of setting up a hunting camp where we could share our passion for hunting. After making the decision to pursue the matter, we looked at several places, one of them being that tract of land in Black Log Valley mentioned in the introduction. When this fell through, the search continued.

Early in December while perusing ads in the Franklin Shopper, a local free paper, I saw one listing a cabin for sale several miles north of Fort Littleton in Huntingdon County. By this time, Chuck had dropped his involvement due to an impending marriage. The other three of us decided to pursue a possible purchase of the cabin, and Pat and I made arrangements to see it.

The cabin was plain with very little in the way of amenities, but we took a walk in the woods close to the cabin and explored the area before making up our minds. Some drawbacks were obvious. The cabin had no water or sewer system. On the positive side, it was situated close enough to Black Log Valley where we were hunting at the time. It was within half an hour of home, which made its frequent use feasible; the cost was affordable; State Game Lands #81 were nearby; and the proximity of the Aughwick Creek, a stocked trout stream, gave promise of fishing opportunities. While walking on the ridge behind the cabin (Lynne's Ridge), we flushed a flock of about twenty turkeys. That convinced us, and we made an offer for the camp. A price of $8,500 was agreed upon, and I gave Mr. George Burkett (the owner) $100 in hand money to seal the deal. Pat and I agreed that if Bill was not interested, we would do the purchase on our own. Bill, however, found the site acceptable and decided to join in. On December 29 of 1986, we met in the office of Mr. Burkett's attorney and signed papers, thus transferring ownership to the three of us.

Within weeks, Camp Bucktail was chosen as the name for the camp. We thought this name to be appropriate since inherent in the name were both hunting and fishing. Later discussions in camp led to one member suggesting that the spelling should have been Bucktale because the deer hunting stories were told over and over, but the chosen name, Bucktail, stuck. I agreed to serve as president, and Pat became treasurer.

Over the ensuing months we began to furnish the cabin. We heated it with a wood/coal summer kitchen stove donated by Pat Haller's mother and supplied light with Coleman lanterns, propane gas lanterns, and kerosene lanterns. We bought a table and chairs from surplus furniture being sold by the Shippensburg Area School District which was closing some elementary schools, due to consolidation. We purchased a set of military surplus bunk beds at Roman's Surplus in Chambersburg. Some additional furniture was donated by members, and we cooked on a Coleman gas stove. Water was hauled from a spring some four miles distant toward Orbisonia. The essentials were in place, and all was ready for our first hunting season.

1987: A Hunting Heritage Begins

The 1987 hunting season was our first in this new camp. Even though we had no experience hunting in this area, fortune did smile upon us. First blood was drawn on opening day of fall turkey season by Pat Haller. Having no prior experience in turkey hunting, Pat dressed in his normal blaze orange hunting apparel, took his thermos of coffee to the top of the ridge behind the cabin, and sat on a log. By noon, boredom had set in. Discouraged by a lack of action, he reached for his thermos to return to the cabin, convinced that the turkeys had won the day. However, a slight crunching sound was heard in the brush above him. Glancing up, he saw three turkeys heading his way. He crawled behind the log and waited until they were closer. With the lead turkey twenty yards away, Pat opened fire, and a flock of about fifteen birds took flight. When the firing ceased, he went up to collect the turkey he was sure he had hit, to find only pellet marks and feathers. Now thoroughly disgusted by this turn of events, Pat picked up his gear for the walk down the ridge. Then the sound of a turkey flopping in the leaves nearby was heard and down over the rocks went the blaze orange clad hunter, firing on the run at the disabled bird. No estimate of the amount of lead in the turkey was ever made, but it had to be considerable based upon the number of shots fired. Camp Bucktail's first turkey kill was recorded.

I made it two turkey kills on the second Saturday of the season. Bill Lloyd and I trekked to the top of the ridge and sat in close proximity to each other. I was experimenting with a newly purchased plunger type turkey call. (Bill somehow resisted the urge to answer.) Suddenly, Bill was stirred from his thoughts by the blast from a nearby twelve gauge. Rushing over to investigate, he found me holding one of the prized birds. I looked at Bill and said, "See how easy this is, Bill." Sometimes it really is easy, but most of the time, as I would find out over the ensuing years, it certainly is not. The bird was a young jake with barely any beard at all, but I was just as pleased as punch over it. Bill's virginity as a turkey hunter remained intact in 1987.

As deer season approached, I drove to the cabin to open it up for the season, only to discover one of the drawbacks of owning a hunting camp. The door was broken and some of the contents were gone, including the lanterns, a kerosene heater, and a fine Queen hunting knife I treasured. New lanterns and another heater were purchased, but spirits were somewhat down because of the break-in. A neighboring cabin belonging to Ray and Carl Alleman was also hit. The perpetrators of the deed were never caught. Some repairs were made, including covering the window portion of the front door with a piece of plywood, installing a new door lock and a deadbolt, and backing the latches with a piece of steel. We hoped that this would make it somewhat harder to break in in the future.

One lesson learned from the event is that you do not leave things in a hunting camp that you value. Thieves break into cabins in hopes of stealing things that they can sell. They know that sometimes camp owners leave such things in camp, even including guns. Nearly thirty years later this lesson was reinforced when a friend's camp was raided. He lost several guns, a chainsaw, and some other valuable items. Also, we have learned that if a cabin is close to a road, thieves burglarize it more frequently. Unfortunately, Camp Bucktail fit that description.

Deer season was spent hunting in Black Log with no kills recorded by members that year. As was becoming our habit, we stayed overnight at camp and drove the twenty or so miles to our favorite hunting area east of the town of Orbisonia. I had taken bucks there in three previous seasons and an occasional doe when I was lucky enough to draw a tag. As was typical of deer hunting during those years, we would see twenty or more does the first day of rifle deer season, but precious few bucks. At that time, we had only the first day and subsequent Saturdays to hunt since we needed to make a living.

One of the things I discovered during the winter following our first hunting season was that going to camp was enjoyable even when no hunting was involved. I coined a name for those winter excursions and wrote several stories about them, calling it doing "winter inventory," since one could determine such things as turkey and deer numbers by observing their tracks in the snow.

1988: Our Second Season In Camp

No harvests were recorded during spring gobbler season. However, fall turkey season came in with great promise. Birds had been sighted on numerous occasions in the pre-season, and memories of 1987 remained fresh. No members of our camp had opportunities, but John Bartholow, hunting as a guest (later to become a member), scored a double kill with a single shot on two young turkeys that crossed in front of him.

As the story goes, we hiked up over Lynne's Ridge that morning and took stands among the plantation of pines and larches that had been planted some twenty or so years before on land owned by the Glatfelter Paper Company. John located at a corner where the larch planting ended and some hardwood forest began. Shortly after dawn broke, a flock of turkeys fed uphill toward him. He focused on one, and when it cleared a copse of trees, he squeezed the trigger. Just as he did, another young bird joined the one at which he was shooting and both dropped, thus exceeding the limit of one bird per season. (I believe the statute of limitations has run out, so the tale can now be told.)

Members of Camp Bucktail fell into a regular pattern of hunting Saturdays and the occasional holiday during archery deer season. Since all of us were teachers, we had the Veterans Day holiday in November to look forward to, and we did take advantage of that. The Thanksgiving vacation gave us a few more days in camp, but we did have to be home for family things. We usually hunted the area on both sides of Lynne's Ridge and the slope of Black Log Mountain across the road. There seemed to be no hunting area that did not involve a substantial climb, so the hunting here would tend to keep us in shape. Luck would not be with us for some time to come, however. The learning curve when hunting a new area can be as steep as the slopes we had to hunt. It took us several years before we experienced regular success at harvesting deer and turkeys, but squirrels were a notable exception. They were plentiful, and a few of us took advantage of that fact.

As usual, we travelled to Black Log to hunt deer, spending the first day of rifle season and the two Saturdays there. No bucks were seen, and since we did not draw a doe tag, no does were taken during the subsequent two-day doe season. I had a flintlock license for the late season over Christmas vacation and spent several days hunting then. On one morning, a herd of does made their way past me, and I recorded my first flintlock kill. Chuck Bailey hunted a few times with us as a guest. We did spend considerable time trying to figure out how to hunt the area on the other side of Lynne's Ridge and noticed that the turkeys seemed to prefer that area. While the gang hunting with Andrew (Junior) Grissinger, who owned the farm on the other side of the ridge, had success in killing deer, we did not. Their success seemed to be primarily because of driving deer. Of course, they had years of experience on their side. They knew what worked and what didn't. We were still on that steep learning curve. Eventually we would get things figured out.

1989: A Learning Year

This turned out to be a great year for us in several ways. During 1988, the Allemans paid the local electric cooperative to run a line to their cabin. At the time, we decided we could not afford the price of buying in, but in the spring of 1989, we decided to wire the cabin. Since I had some past experience as an electrician, I volunteered to do the wiring. A number of friends and neighbors showed up to help. Steve Grissinger, who lives near the camp, aided me. He did most of the work on the service entrance. Junior, who was Steve's father, kept the work party entertained with his wit. He was quick to point out that if we'd had lights the previous fall, he wouldn't have bruised his shins the night of the break-in. Fred Gunnell, another neighbor with experience as an electrician, provided guidance and encouragement. We finished the service entrance and installed a circuit breaker box and one ground fault receptacle. This made it possible for an inspector to certify our work so we could begin to get electricity. The electric company then connected us to their power lines. We then finished the wiring by installing lights and receptacles. With power being available, Bill Lloyd rounded up an electric stove for the camp and Sam Norris, principal at Shippensburg High School, donated an old refrigerator.

In late summer and early fall, the ridge behind the cabin was clear-cut. All agreed that positive effects upon hunting might result as new growth would likely provide better cover on the ridge itself.

Fall turkey season appeared to be a lost cause until the final day of the season. I arrived in camp before dark on Friday evening and did a walkabout. While on top of Lynne's Ridge, I heard a flock of turkeys going to roost on the flat below. That night when the rest of the gang arrived, a plan was hatched. The next morning, we hiked over the ridge and set up in places we thought the turkeys might go to when they came down from their roost. My planned spot was at the pine tree on the corner of the larch plantation, and that happened to be right where the flock headed when they flew down off the roost. I took the first bird to show his blue head. Shortly after that, my son-in-law, Crawford Peters, ambushed a bird. He was set up on the hillside above the larches and made a nice shot. Jack Stayer, father-in-law of guest John Bartholow, also was successful. Three turkeys in one morning was the best we had ever done. While a "hero" shot of the three of us was taken, it was lost when the only copy of the logbook at the time burned in the 2012 fire. It is a shame not to have it here, as such events should be remembered.

Deer season was split between hunting in the vicinity of the cabin and Black Log. We decided to give the area of the cabin a try for the first day of buck season. Chuck Bailey, still hunting as a guest, took the first cabin buck while hunting on top of Lynne's Ridge. It was a five-point. In December, membership in the camp expanded to four partners when John Bartholow bought into the camp. Crawford and I harvested does during antlerless deer season while hunting in Black Log. No kills were recorded during muzzleloader season. John, Pat, and I did some exploration of the big mountain and found several good areas that had potential for hunting both deer and turkeys. On one expedition, John walked the spine of the ridge, and I dropped downhill a few hundred yards. Each of us saw bucks, and some of them were pretty nice ones. Between us, we probably sighted over thirty deer.

Chuck Bailey with the camp's first buck

1990: *Things Keep Getting Better*

Spring gobbler season remained an unproductive season one more time, although extensive efforts were expended. Pat, John, and I hunted every available day, but could not find any gobblers to call in. Late one morning while I drove around the ridge, I saw a huge gobbler crossing the road near what the locals call Indian Hill. I tried to get ahead of him and call him in without success.

The summer months saw Pat and John contributing their efforts to install a new window in the bunkroom to provide ventilation and a possible escape route in the event of fire. The roof was also coated with paint. Chuck Bailey donated a baseboard electric heating unit which he took from his home during remodeling. I once again served as resident electrician for the camp. The single unit of electric baseboard was adequate to heat the cabin, but because of expense, we continued to use the wood burning stove as our primary source of heat.

Archery season arrived with great expectations, as deer were being seen and plenty of sign was in evidence. Pat, who was on sabbatical leave from his teaching duties, was able to spend extra days at camp. He saw a fair number of deer and spotted turkey flocks with regularity. Although no deer were taken during archery season, Pat managed to miss a six-point and a four-point within an hour's time on the back side of the ridge at the northwest corner of the larch plantation. On several occasions, I saw a three-point at the feeder behind the camp in the pre-season.

Fall turkey season proved profitable for two hunters from camp. John and Crawford harvested turkeys on the opening day. No other turkey kills were recorded, although we encountered them regularly. We spent a lot of time hunting squirrels with plenty of success during small game season. I killed a bunch and parted them out. They went into a pot of squirrel stew for the opening of buck season.

Buck season found the members split for opening day. Pat joined John in John's native Bedford County hunting haunts rather than hunting the area of the cabin even though he had seen numerous bucks in the previous weeks. Another "bucktale" was added when Crawford took a six-point buck on the first day of rifle season while hunting on the back side of the ridge from a blind that Pat had constructed. It was wounded by one of the Grissinger hunters, and Crawford finished it off. On the first Friday of buck season, Pat and I took personal days and returned to the camp to try our luck. Pat had that luck about 4:30 PM in the vicinity of the game lands parking lot. After dragging the deer to his truck and returning to camp, he was able to con me into field dressing the deer by claiming exhaustion. I obliged, but both of us agreed that the story would probably be embellished through time. Unfortunately, no camera being available, no photo of Pat and his buck exists.

Crawford and I continued to hunt the area in subsequent weeks, but to no avail, although deer were spotted on occasion. It would appear that hunting for deer might prove to be good in the future when members of our camp have learned this area better and as growth replaced clear-cut areas of the ridge. More deer had been seen, especially bucks, in 1990 than in any previous year since the purchase of the camp. Hope springs eternal, or some such, and seemed to be improving. We had taken three bucks in the past two seasons.

Crawford Peters with the second Camp Bucktail buck

1991: *Camp Is A Great Place To Be*

Spring gobbler season once again proved to be unproductive for all hunters from the camp. Signs remained good, turkeys were sighted, and a few near misses were recorded, but meat was not put on the table. There actually were three different flocks in our area. It was amazing that nobody got one, but we continued to learn.

Archery season opened with reasonable expectations. The clear-cut area of the ridge continued to develop with brush, and numerous deer had been sighted on various scouting excursions prior to the season. No kills were reported in the season and no blood was drawn. However, I managed to lose a few arrows while hunting the ridge. Chuck, hunting again as a guest of the camp, had deer within shooting distance on the ridge, but was unable to get off a shot as he was caught napping. John and Pat did not hunt the cabin area to any great extent. Sightings of turkeys were made, and the anticipation built for the opening of turkey season.

Turkey season opened on November 2. Pat and Bill were absent on opening day. Pre-season scouting disclosed that there were not many turkeys around camp. John and Jack Stayer kept me company as the season dawned. That morning, none of us saw any turkeys, so during the noon lunch break, I switched to blaze orange to do some squirrel hunting on the top of the ridge near the point. John and Jack continued to hunt turkeys without success. Later in the afternoon, a flight of turkeys approached from the southeastern end of Black Log Mountain, which the locals call Gobblers Knob. The flock landed just over the lip of the ridge from me. After making a few yelps and putts with my push button turkey call, one of the birds came within range. I opened fire. The bird flopped its way down nearly to the bottom of the ridge, thus carrying it to camp became much easier.

A week later saw five of us in camp. I was joined by Pat, John, Jack, and Pat's son-in-law, Rob Reed. Pat and I started the day on the mountain to scout for deer while hunting turkeys. John, Jack, and Rob decided to hunt on the back side of the ridge only to encounter numerous other

The easy turkey

hunters who had been putting pressure on the area all week. No shots were fired and no turkeys were seen until Pat, who had worked his way over to Lynne's Ridge, spotted what he thought was a stump. When the "stump," which turned out to be a turkey, attempted to take flight, he downed it with a single shot. The score now stood at two smallish turkeys for camp after the second week.

Although no additional kills were recorded on turkeys, John and I spent the last weekend scouting the high mountain for deer while Pat worked the lower area of the mountain. Each of us reported seeing a large number of deer, including several rack bucks. It seemed that hunting on top of the mountain might offer the best chance for us, but that mountain is steep. One certainly worked up a sweat getting there.

Buck season opened on December 2 with Pat, Chuck, and myself in camp. Chuck hunted as a guest. John returned to his native Bedford for buck season, and Bill was unable to hunt due to the impending birth of his second son. Chuck and I hunted the game lands above Alleman's cabin, while Pat opted to hunt the area above the game lands parking lot. Steady rain throughout the day made for less than optimal hunting conditions. I missed a rack buck early in the morning and to this day I can't figure out how. It was one of those situations that leave one scratching his head. I had an easy broadside shot at the buck. Perhaps a twig got in the way and deflected the bullet. Chuck did not miss. He downed a half-racked buck that would have been a six-point if one of his antlers had not been broken off.

My 1991 six-point

On the first Friday of rifle deer season, Pat and I took personal days and returned to camp for another try. Hunting separately, we planned to meet mid-morning, climb the mountain, and try a two-man drive across the top. Having missed making contact at the appropriate hour, Pat climbed the mountain looking for me. I stayed at the base of the foot rocks waiting for Pat. When Pat returned to the cabin, he found a six-point hanging. As it happened, one of my neighbors from Saint Thomas, Rich Forbes, missed the buck close to the road some distance below me around noon. I waited patiently after being alerted by the shot, and shortly, I saw motion in the brush below me. That motion turned into a deer, and he had antlers. When he came into the open, my .300 Weatherby cracked.

Meat was on the ground. This was the first buck taken at "my rock," a stand on the game lands located above Alleman's cabin. The rock, after which the stand is named, is a huge boulder about the size and shape of a Volkswagen beetle. A few years later, I made a seat by piling several smaller flat rocks in front of the big rock, and it became one of my favorite spots on Black Log Mountain. In the future, several more bucks would be harvested there.

While leaving the cabin on Saturday morning, Pat waited for a truck to pass him before crossing the road. A loud thump was heard as the truck approached. Walking down the road, Pat discovered that a spike buck had committed suicide by taking a swan dive off the upper bank into the side of the pickup. We helped the guy and his son field dress the deer, and they took it home. Another full day of hunting in the mountain proved fruitless again for Pat. No deer were sighted on the last Saturday either, so the final deer season tally for camp stood at Chuck-1, George-1, pickup truck-1, and Pat-0.

1992: Things Continue To Improve

The 1992 hunting season began on May 2 with the spring gobbler season. John, Pat, and I made the call to arms, but no turkeys were sighted on the opening day. Numerous contacts with deer were made. Pat counted sixteen. Although many hours were spent in the woods throughout the month, the spring season ended once more without a turkey kill being recorded.

As archery season approached in the fall, expectations were on the rise. I had made a number of scouting trips over the summer and reported several sightings of rack bucks. The writer of this history was remiss in not keeping accurate records for the year. At least two events worthy of note occurred, however.

John, who was on sabbatical leave, hit a six-point. After three hours of tracking by John and me, the trail ran out. The deer presumably survived. Pat managed to keep the comic side of deer hunting alive when he was surprised by a four-point after laying his bow down to answer the call of nature. It remained in shooting distance for about forty minutes, but stayed in thick cover. The buck left the area when John and I came down off the ridge top. Pat never did get a shot. No kills were recorded during archery season.

Of equal concern was that for some reason, no turkeys had been seen during archery season. When turkey season opened, those concerns proved to be well founded. No sightings at all were reported. For the first time since purchasing our cabin, turkey season was a complete washout.

Pat, Chuck, Bill, Bill's brother Craig, and I were present for the first day of buck season. John again hunted in Bedford County. Bill and Craig stayed on Lynne's Ridge. The rest of us hunted the big mountain. I hunted lower on the mountain with Pat near a place where deer cross the road from Lynne's Ridge. Neither of us saw any deer, so at 11:00, I left Pat and hiked to a stand I had scouted out above Alleman's cabin. It was located several hundred yards above my favorite rock, previously mentioned. This stand provided cover, being behind a blowdown on the last bench before the top of the mountain. I picked this spot from which to hunt because during archery season I had seen a rack buck there. A short time after arriving, a buck emerged from a thicket to my left at a distance of about sixty to seventy yards. My only shot was as the buck was going straight away from me. Lousy aim, but a good blood trail. I followed the deer for about half a mile or more until I got a walking broadside shot. After this second shot, the buck was mine.

As I remember it, the buck went downhill from where I had the first shot and made its way along the bench closest to the road below. He continued eastward until he apparently saw a lone hunter sitting on a log below. Then he turned uphill, thus presenting me with that broadside shot. (That lone hunter turned out to be the son of a state policeman whom I encountered several times during subsequent years on the first day of buck season.) The four-point had unusual antlers with heavy main beams, but only brow tines for additional points. In later years with the advent of antler restrictions, he would not have been a legal buck. In 1992, he was, and I was happy with him. Everyone saw some deer, but this became the only buck taken by us that entire season. At least we kept our string of buck kills alive.

My 1992 four-point's antlers reside on the wall of my den.

Pat hunted alone the first Friday and saw nothing. Chuck and Pat, with my assistance as driver, returned to the woods the first Saturday, but again, no antlers were sighted. While Pat and I took a noontime break at the cabin, a group of hunters, probably hunting with the Grissingers, drove the ridge. As we watched, a herd of a dozen does ran down from the ridge behind the cabin and crossed the road. As this was not yet antlerless deer season, they continued on in safety. No more deer were seen the rest of the day.

1993: The Bears Arrive

Spring gobbler season again proved futile as the turkeys were totally absent. No acceptable reason was determined for this, but not one turkey was sighted during the season.

Bear sightings!!! On July 9, Pat and I spent the night at the cabin in anticipation of doing some work the next day. About 8:00 AM, while drinking coffee, Pat glanced out the rear window and saw a young bear at the feeder. The bear's weight was estimated at 150 to 175 pounds. We watched him for nearly an hour. Unfortunately, no cameras were on hand. This turned out to be the year our Pennsylvania black bear population completed a period of expansion into more southern areas of our state. In subsequent years, bears could be found in every county of the state, including even the city of Philadelphia. Prior to this year, one had to travel to the north central mountains to find them.

All camp members spent some time in camp the next few months. The main objective was to see bears, and that objective was certainly met. On Saturday, July 17, Pat arrived at the cabin just before dark to set up for another bear watch. He heard rustling in the trees up the hill while he was unloading the truck and sensed a presence other than deer. After unloading the truck, but prior to unpacking, he flipped on the floodlight and watched as a large mother bear and her cub walked down to the feeder. Mother and cub proceeded to feed while Pat captured the scene on videotape. At one point, the bears were spooked by something below the cabin, and Mama went to investigate. Both returned to the feeder and stayed until close to 10:00 PM. Before he went to bed, Pat flipped on the light one more time and saw another bear, possibly the same bear that was the first one seen a week earlier. Numerous bear watches continued throughout the summer, and members were rewarded with some great sightings. Many photographs were taken, but they were lost when the camp scrapbook burned in the fire of 2012.

Fall hunting season began with archery, but the first two weeks proved to be unsuccessful. I saw a decent flock of turkeys on the second weekend, so this raised hopes for that coming season. On October 23, during the third week of the season, Pat, Chuck, and I hunted the back side of the ridge in the morning, and all of us witnessed a welcome sight. A flock of about thirty turkeys entertained us during the early hours, confirming the hope that the turkeys were back after a two-year absence. For the afternoon hunt, all three of us moved to the big mountain behind Alleman's cabin. Chuck was rewarded with a doe of about eighty pounds, his first kill with the bow. The deer was taken high in the rocks toward Gobblers Knob, half a mile from the cabin.

Early in November, members of the cabin met to vote on accepting Chuck for full membership and to discuss building an addition, as with five members, more space would be needed. The vote accepting Chuck was unanimous. His skills in the building trades would certainly be useful during the following years. Preliminary plans for that addition were also discussed with construction to begin during the following summer.

Buck season opened on November 29 with Chuck, Pat and me taking to the woods. John, as usual, went back to Bedford County to hunt. Pat and I also hunted the first Friday and Saturday. No bucks were spotted, and no kills recorded. On the first day of doe season while hunting alone, I took a doe about a hundred yards above Alleman's cabin. The doe was by itself and made the fatal mistake of crossing the logging road about fifty yards below me. One shot from the .30-06, and meat was on the ground.

Muzzleloader season opened on December 27. Pat and I were in camp. Pat took a stand at the corner where the larch plantation and hardwoods meet. I walked down the road to Indian Hill (so named by the locals) and put on a drive. Two does crossed near Pat, and he cut loose a blast from his flintlock rifle, which he had named "Old Gert." One of the does lurched, indicating a hit. When I arrived on the scene, we took up the blood trail which led us across the top of the ridge and all the way into the Aughwick Creek, where I found the doe attempting to cross. After the doe was dispatched in the middle of the creek, I waded into the frigid water to retrieve it. Pat went back to the camp and returned with his pickup truck to haul the doe and one nearly frozen wader back to camp. The fire in the wood stove was warm and the beer from the refrigerator cold. Both agreed that this was a great way to end a hunting season. While no bucks were taken, we did harvest two does.

What follows is an attempt to fill in some details from our log of camp kills for the years 1994 through 1998. No yearly stories are available. They were lost when my computer crashed during 1998. Unfortunately, no backup copy was saved. We also lost a great many photographs from that time. Only a few have survived.

1994: Camp Membership Changes

After a simply horrid winter with four months of seemingly unending snow and cold temperatures, I retired from teaching in June of 1994 and resolved to spend every day possible hunting from then on. I remember saying to my wife Doris, "I'm going to hunt every day that the law allows." She replied, "Well, get it out of your system." In the years following, I have to admit that I have slowed down somewhat, but the bug still has me.

That fall, John harvested the first gobbler taken at the cabin, a big bird with an 11½ inch beard. He had set up on Black Log Mountain above Alleman's cabin. Upon hearing several birds gobble, he called one of them in.

The only deer taken was a doe I got during archery season while still hunting along the spine of Lynne's Ridge. As I worked my way along the spine of the ridge, she crossed fifteen yards in front of me, presenting a "can't miss" shot. Dragging a deer downhill toward camp directly below the kill site is an easy chore. The last thirty yards uphill to camp when one is tired can be slightly more of a job.

Pat, one of the original founding members of Camp Bucktail, decided to sell his share and leave the camp. The rest of us bought him out and, since we were down to four members again, the planned addition became unnecessary. The chronology of events leading to this was lost when the camp logbook burned in 2012.

Since I had retired, and since I had been reading outdoor magazines for decades, I thought it was time for me to go on some of those hunting trips to exotic places I dreamed about all those years. Actually, the first big game trip happened during August of 1991, a caribou hunt to northern Quebec. I returned home from that hunt with two caribou bulls. In September of 1994, I went on the second one, a moose hunt in the wilds of northern Alberta, and took a really nice bull moose. A few weeks later, I went to Ontario on an unsuccessful bear hunt. These three were the first of well over sixty hunting trips that I worked into my schedule, thus taking some time away from my hunting camps in Pennsylvania. The stories of a number of those hunting trips are told in my two previously published books.

1995: Our First Eight-Point Bites The Dust

During fall of 1995, I hunted nearly every day of archery and small game season except for days with really lousy weather, but didn't take much game. An exception would have been squirrels, which I hunted with my old Savage .22. On one day, I went grouse hunting with a neighbor, Bill Livesey, and his friend Bob. While hunting on top of the big mountain, we took two grouse and must have missed twenty or so. After missing one bird, Bill remarked, "I just wanted to let him know I was in the area." Sometimes a miss is the best we can do.

For some strange reason, the usual flocks of turkeys had, once again, located elsewhere, so turkey season came and went without any of us harvesting a bird. Over the course of small game season, I managed to take over two dozen squirrels. These were parted out and frozen so I could make them into a stew for deer season.

Buck season found Bill Lloyd and his brother Craig in camp along with Chuck, Craig's army buddy Scott, and myself. The Sunday before season opener, we cooked a huge pot of squirrel stew which vanished before the sun went down. My working up a pot of one type of stew or another became a tradition in camp. Not a bad tradition to maintain.

On the first day of buck season, the guys all headed out for stands they had chosen. I decided to hunt from my favorite stand at the rock above Alleman's cabin. About 8:00 AM, I spied movement to my right and downhill close to the property line. That movement soon disclosed a pair of does followed by a nice eight-point buck. The does left to head downhill toward Alleman's cabin, but the buck, as bucks sometimes do, stayed put to watch them go. When he took a step forward and exposed his shoulder to me, I made a one-shot kill. Once again, the drag to camp was all downhill and an easy one. Scott also had an opportunity at a buck but did not connect. The other guys hunted on the two Saturdays of rifle season with me attempting to drive deer to them. I did push some deer past them, but no bucks were seen. Mine ended up being the only deer taken that year.

As had become tradition, all of the camp members got together after Christmas for flintlock season. I had no tags, so I served as driver for them. Several shots were taken, but no blood was drawn, and no meat was put into freezers. While the weather in late December can be very cold, the cabin was warm. It was nice to return from a cold day of hunting to a warm cabin.

1996: Squirrels And Turkeys Abound, But Very Few Deer

This year, the turkeys returned with a vengeance. At least three flocks were seen in the area from time to time, presumably because of a bumper crop of acorns. John harvested another nice gobbler with a ten-inch beard. Chuck and I took fall hens. Turkey hunting is John's forte. He certainly has had more success at it than the rest of us. I remember that I took my fall bird from a small flock I called, "my regulars." Nearly every evening at the same time, they would roost in the trees at the base of the foot rocks. I ambushed them one evening and took a nice young bird for Thanksgiving dinner. Chuck got his in the area of the hollow above what is now Terry Dennis's home.

A fox squirrel on a poplar tree on Black Log Mountain

Squirrel hunting was excellent, and a few fox squirrels began to appear in the area, especially on the big mountain. They are larger than the grey squirrels and have a different alarm bark. I wanted to take one to mount for my trophy room, but did not get that job done.

Deer hunting was tough. For some reason, it seemed that there just were not all that many deer around. I don't have any notes and no particular memories of that buck season, so this is a short yearly story. Nobody got a buck. It is probable that nobody even saw one.

During doe season, I made the only camp kill, taking a button buck while hunting on the other side of Lynne's Ridge from a stand above the larches. As I remember it, I was in a blind Crawford had put together some years before. It was located on the hillside above the larch plantation. Things were fairly quiet most of the morning, but about mid-morning I heard a gunshot. Shortly thereafter, a deer appeared running along the upper margin of the larches, and I took it with a single shot. I remember being a bit disappointed at having taken a button buck, but in later years have realized that this is not a tragedy at all. Button bucks are good eating, and it is the does that have fawns. Therefore, it may be better to take a button buck than a mature doe. Besides, as my wife Doris says, "You can't eat antlers."

1997: *Our Second Spring Gobbler Goes Into The Books*

May of 1997 brought our camp's second spring gobbler kill. I called in a mature gobbler while hunting at the upper edge of the larches on the other side of Lynne's Ridge. When I set up in the morning, a flock of crows flew into the area and raised a ruckus. The gobbler sounded off, I guess to let the crows know who was boss. I waited for the sky to get brighter and then gave a coming down cackle and a few feeding clucks. Within minutes, a huge gobbler showed up. When his head went behind a tree, I got into position to shoot. As he emerged, I shot, and he flopped. The bird was a big one with an eleven-inch beard and one inch spurs. He weighed about twenty pounds. This is proof that blind hogs do find the occasional acorn.

During archery season in October, I harvested a doe while hunting from a ladder stand close to the gap on the state game lands boundary line. Shortly after dawn, a group of five does fed past my stand. I picked out one that gave me a good clear shot and cut an arrow lose. The arrow went through both lungs, and the doe left a blood trail anyone could have followed. As I remember, it looked as if someone had taken a can of red paint and sprayed it out on both sides of her path. Another downhill drag and some great eating.

Buck season came and went with the result that nobody saw a buck. Bill Lloyd took a doe while hunting in Franklin County. That was the total for this particular year.

As had become a common occurrence, I visited camp quite frequently during the following winter. I was most interested in doing winter inventory when the ground would be covered with fresh snow and the woods could be read like a newspaper. It was evident that while we were not all that successful at killing deer, there were plenty of them in the area. Tracks do not lie. Coyotes also left tracks in the snow, but it was evident there were not as many as most hunters seem to think.

On a typical winter trip to camp, I arrive early in the evening, fire up the wood burner, and settle in to enjoy a foamer or two. I have no trouble getting up in the mornings before dawn, so no alarm is needed. After a breakfast of coffee, oatmeal, and some fruit, I usually set out for a walk. Sometimes that walk would take me up on the big mountain and sometimes across Lynne's Ridge to the larch plantation. I then return to camp late in the morning and work up a lunch. After a nap, I might go out for a second walk, and this time I would hike up the ridge I had not visited in the AM. One thing that worried me again this particular winter was I did not find much sign of turkeys. This was prophetic, as the coming season later proved to be tough where turkeys were concerned.

1998: A Mercy Killing Year

Again, the turkeys chose other areas in which to live and were absent from our area, so spring gobbler season was a total washout. Chuck and John decided to hunt in Path Valley on land one of their fellow teachers had access to, and they found birds. I found nothing in the area of camp, but it was not for lack of trying.

Fall came with what appeared to be an increase in the deer population. Hopes were high. I saw deer regularly, but none presented shots during archery season. One morning while hunting at the rock, I saw a young buck that appeared to have been injured. He limped severely, not having the use of one of his hind legs. I resolved to take him if I could, but did not have an opportunity to do so until rifle season. On the first day, he crossed the logging road above camp, and I took him with a single shot. He ran downhill and ended up less than a hundred yards from the cabin. It would be the only deer taken at camp this year. (I wrote a story about this which follows. It has previously been published, but I made some changes for this tome.)

ON THE SUBJECT OF TROPHY HUNTING AND MERCY KILLING

The last Friday morning of the 1998 archery deer season started as usual with a twenty-minute hike from the cabin to a rock high on Black Log Mountain that I found some years ago. This rock is about the size of a Volkswagen beetle. I made a seat in front of it by stacking two flat rocks in such a way that I could sit high enough to shoot my bow without standing up. Since I discovered this spot, it has yielded four bucks in rifle season and had afforded me numerous opportunities for bucks and does during archery season. I came there that morning to hunt only bucks, as the rut was in full swing and they were acting really crazy.

I made my early morning hike in complete darkness. It seemed important to get there before the deer. Since it would be a good twenty minutes until dawn broke, I took my time settling in and arranging everything for easy access. My bow leaned against a sapling within easy reach with an arrow nocked and ready. After donning my camouflage facemask and gloves and removing my grunt call from my backpack, I was as ready as I could be. Now if the deer would only cooperate.

As shadowy semi-darkness slowly replaced the dark night sky, I became aware of things moving in my part of the woods. The first to be identified gave me a real start. An arm's length away, a five-foot blacksnake slithered by me in search of breakfast. I let him pass undisturbed. As he moved downhill, a chipmunk noticed him and the alarm was sounded. Suddenly the woods came alive with the shrill barks of these tiny forest dwellers. For the next fifteen minutes or so, they kept up their chatter until the intruder made its way out of sight. I could follow the snake's progress by the racket they raised.

Shortly, the grey squirrels emerged to feed upon the abundant acorns. This had been a really productive year for the oaks, and the nutritious nuts could be found everywhere. Life for a squirrel is a struggle for survival. It alternates between feast and famine. They were now taking advantage of the feast part. I think a squirrel makes more noise than a deer, and these certainly caused a distraction. It was not yet fully daylight. Not a breath of air moved on this nearly perfect morning. Where were the deer?

All of a sudden, my eyes detected motion to my left. A deer trotted along the bench below the rock and to my right. Its path would bring it within the magic twenty-yard limit. The adrenaline surge caused me to breathe much harder, and my heart felt as though it would pound right out of my chest when I got my first good look at him. I thought, "It's a buck!" I could make out two points coming off one main beam. If he had brow tines, he would be an eight-point. Now I was really excited.

Just before he moved into range, he turned uphill to his right, putting him on a course that would take him past me at too great a distance for a shot. I blew softly on the grunt call, and he slid to a stop. I grunted again. He stood his ground, looking for the other buck that was challenging him. I took a chance and made a doe bleat. With fire in his eyes, he sped toward me on a dead run and stopped less than ten yards away. I hadn't picked up my bow yet, so I had a real Mexican standoff on my hands.

The camo pattern I wore did the job perfectly. So long as I remained motionless, the buck had no clue I was there, but he had me pinned. After what seemed like an hour or so but was in reality only a couple of minutes, he turned to his left and walked slowly away from me. When his head disappeared behind a large oak, I picked up my bow. Decision time had come.

As he faced me, I noticed that his rack sported only five points. One antler had three and the other, two. There were no brow tines. This buck did not meet the standards I had set for myself this year, so when he passed below me at a distance of twenty yards, I did not pull the trigger. I think he was completely unaware of how close his brush with death had been, and so totally into the rut that he didn't care.

Since retiring in 1994, I had resolved to shoot nothing but decent sized bucks. I guess that made me a trophy hunter. It was not something I was proud of, but just the way I thought at that time. I hunt at least two and sometimes three states for whitetails each year, and I harvest my share. My wife and I eat very little beef or pork, for venison is plentiful, and the freezer is usually well supplied with it. I will take a doe for meat, but mature bucks held a special attraction. I later mellowed in that regard and became less picky as I got older.

As the morning went on, several does and two smaller bucks passed the stand. Both of the bucks responded to the grunt and bleat calls I used. I took no shots, even though the smallest buck, a three point, was a cripple. At the time, I had no idea how this buck had been injured, but after he passed, I had second thoughts. It was obvious to me that, in his condition, he would never survive the coming winter. I began to regret not taking him.

Sometimes life gives one a second chance to remedy a bad decision. This came during buck season. I sat on a different stand that morning. Fifteen minutes into the legal hunting day, the same crippled youngster crossed the logging road below me. This time it took me only a few seconds to make up my mind. His tortured existence ended with a well-placed neck shot.

An hour later, I had the young buck hung on the camp meat pole. As I skinned him, I found that his right leg was broken and an infection had set in. Most of the meat was fine. I had to discard only a small portion from the stifle joint downward. Being curious, I carefully dissected that leg, trying to determine what had caused the injury. The tibia (shinbone) had fractured in two places, and the femur was broken just above the knee. The splintered end of the tibia had penetrated the skin. It must have been a painful injury indeed. I can only surmise that a car had hit him some time before our first encounter. The fact that he was still getting around is testimony to the will deer have to survive.

While my 1998 buck was no wall-hanger, I felt better about taking him than had I let him go and waited for a bigger buck. Sometimes you have to do what you think is right. Next year is another year. Maybe I'll hold out for an eight-point then.

1999: Paybacks Are Hell

Spring gobbler season arrived, and several camp members hunted hard and frequently, but took no birds. The highlight of the season occurred on the second Saturday. John and I were in camp to make war on gobblers. I left camp before dawn and made my way to the logging road, intending to cross over the ridge and set up ambush for the turkeys on the edge of the clear-cut. John drove his truck around the end of the ridge, planning to hunt the backside of Lynne's Ridge.

Just as I left the road to go into the woods, I saw a truck enter the cabin driveway. Thinking that one of two things was happening, and both of those would be bad things, I returned to the cabin to investigate. When I got there, I found out that the cabin was not being burglarized. That was the good news. The bad news was that John had drawn blood. Unfortunately, it was not turkey blood. He had jammed his shotgun, and while attempting to dislodge the stuck round, plunged his knife into the meat of his hand. At the time, there was no first aid kit in camp, so we went to the Grissinger farm to see if they could provide some first aid stuff. With a bit of patching, John eventually drove to the emergency ward at Bedford Hospital for professional treatment of his wound. Not wishing to waste a good opportunity, I later made fun of John's accident.

On the second Saturday, Chuck and Larry Dubbs, who we knew from his years as one of the maintenance staff at the Shippensburg Area School District, had a close encounter of the black, furry kind while hunting in Hull Holtry's backyard. Mr. Holtry also worked as a custodian at Shippensburg High School for a number of years, so we knew him fairly well. The guys had set up on the edge of a field to call turkeys, but nothing was coming to their calls or decoys. Later when they approached the Holtry house, Mrs. Holtry asked, "Did you see the bear?" It had entered the field just around a corner where they could not see it.

Fall hunting began with archery deer season. This year it was exceptional with the hunters seeing good numbers of deer and an adequate supply of bucks. On the first Saturday, I scored on a nice doe above the Alleman cabin. Chuck had gone on a hike along the game lands boundary above me and spooked some deer, sending a herd of six down to me. One shot from my tree stand and the string of kills was kept alive for another year.

Larry Dubbs, dressed in full blaze orange, killed his first turkey on the opening day of fall turkey season at his favorite spot near the property line on top of the ridge above the cabin. A "herd" of two turkeys bent on committing suicide hove upon the scene. One shot from Larry's scattergun dispatched a volunteer, and this turkey became a part of camp history.

The Sunday before buck season Chuck Bailey, Bill Lloyd, the Dubbs clan (including Larry's son Bill), and I were in camp for the purpose of sampling the traditional game stew, sighting in our rifles, and perhaps doing some scouting. The stew, as usual, disappeared quickly. We all retired that night to sleep it off, with the usual dreams of big bucks.

The next morning, we made our separate ways into the woods. I ended up high in the rocks above Alleman's cabin. Soon after the sun rose, a small group of deer appeared. One of them was a unicorn spike which I felled with a single shot. In the process of field dressing this buck, I discovered that paybacks truly are hell. Being an experienced woodsman and having taught numerous youngsters hunting safety, I violated one of my own rules. After making the initial incision from the middle of the abdomen to the breastbone, I made the final cut to the pelvis toward myself, while holding the buck's hind legs apart with my legs. As in the case of John Bartholow the past spring, stupidity truly does run clean to the bone. The knife slipped, and I managed to plunge it into my calf right up to the hilt. When I finally returned to camp with the buck and a boot filled with my blood, only Larry Dubbs was present. As I had quite enough of this particular buck, I gave it to Larry and left for home to get medical treatment for my wound. More could be said, but reporting this should be sufficient. Needless to say, I no longer make fun of John about his knife wound.

During muzzleloader season, Larry Dubbs, hunting again from his favorite spot above the cabin, made his first muzzleloader kill, a nice tender doe. In summary, lots of game was seen, and hopes were high for the next year.

2000: *Plan B Is Sometimes The Best Plan*

Spring gobbler season came upon us with plentiful supplies of gobblers. On a scouting trip in April, Nick Sabetto and I observed ten gobblers along the edge of John's favorite hollow. The birds seemed to be using the clear cut for strutting early in the mornings. On the first day, several gobblers were seen, but nobody killed one. Larry was the only hunter to have shooting, this resulting in a clean miss.

The following Monday, I was alone in camp. My plan was to hike over the ridge behind camp and set up along the clear cut below Crawford's stand. I never got there. On the way up the hill to the logging road, I heard a gobbler sounding off on the big mountain. On the second gobble, I decided the heck with plan A and went to plan B. Hiking rapidly up the mountain, I got to a blowdown along the game lands boundary near my favorite rock above Alleman's cabin and settled in, the gobbler never ceasing his gobbling. I gave a coming down cackle and several feeding clucks, and was answered by not one, but two gobblers. I called one more time, then stopped calling. So did the gobblers. About ten minutes later, I saw a turkey approaching from down the ridge. As it got closer, I could see that it had a beard, and the red on its head confirmed that it was a gobbler, which made him a legal target. When his head disappeared behind a tree, I raised my shotgun. As the bird emerged, I squeezed the trigger, and my spring gobbler season was over. This was to be the only gobbler harvested during spring. Upon close examination, he had all three colors on his head; red, white, and blue, making him a most patriotic bird. I had him mounted in flying position, and he hangs from the ceiling of my living room. (I wrote another story about this bird, entitled THE MILLENNIUM GOBBLER. It is included in my first book of hunting stories, THE LUCKIEST HUNTER ALIVE).

As usual, fall activity began with archery deer season. Chuck was first to score, harvesting a big doe at the point of the ridge. As Chuck related it, the doe was with a fawn, and he drew his bow at least three times before getting the killing shot. Some days, you are just supposed to kill a deer, aren't you? My archery season turned out to be a good one. I took two does. This was the first time I have killed two deer in one archery deer season. Additionally, I got both while sneak hunting. The first was taken on top of the ridge above the cabin. I sneaked up on three deer bedded down and when one stood up, my arrow struck it right behind the shoulder. About a week later while hunting on the big mountain, I was returning to camp when a doe crossed the road in front of me and began to feed in the woods below. As it moved into the clear, another well-placed arrow harvested doe number two. Both deer were killed with the same arrow, another unusual circumstance.

Turkeys were really scarce again that fall. I hunted the entire bow season and saw only five turkeys. Chuck, when bow hunting in the rocks on the high mountain, saw twelve. We wondered what happened to all the turkeys that seemed to be everywhere in the spring.

One morning while hunting high on the last bench before the laurel, a big ten-point passed my stand at too great a distance for a good shot. I saw this buck several times later in the same spot and felt I had him patterned.

Buck season arrived. Chuck, Bill Lloyd, Bill Dubbs, Larry Dubbs, and I were in camp for the first day. We all saw lots of deer, with Larry Dubbs missing a nice rack buck and me eyeballing a spike (not quite legal). Larry saw at least one more rack buck while walking back to the cabin. Chuck encountered a bunch of hunters where he intended to hunt, so he moved to a different spot which turned out to be unproductive. As an aside, the huge ten-point I thought I had patterned during archery season was killed by Ernie, one of the hunters who hunted out of the Alleman cabin. He had taken a stand close to their camp and shot the buck as he crossed from Lynne's Ridge on to the mountain, intercepting it before the buck got to me. I had an opportunity to take a legal spike the second day, but decided not to pull the trigger. Hindsight says this was a dumb move. Oh well, there was still muzzleloader season. Bill and Larry Dubbs hunted most of the first week with me. Nobody scored, but we had a good time anyway.

Muzzleloader season saw everyone who was healthy, with the exception of Bill Lloyd (who had duty with the National Guard that week), in camp. I also missed this season due to a medical problem. Deer were sighted every day, and everyone who hunted got a shot. No blood was drawn and no deer harvested. This is still one of the best seasons to hunt whether or not game is taken, and I hated missing it.

2001: *In Sickness And In Health*

In January, I traveled to Idaho to hunt mountain lion and took a nice tom cat. It ended up being large enough to qualify for listing in the Boone and Crockett record book and was at the time the number five mountain lion in the Safari Club record book.

Spring gobbler season arrived with very few gobblers having been seen in the area around the cabin. As a result, Chuck and John again decided to hunt with a fellow teacher from Shippensburg who had access to land in Path Valley. Chuck scored on a nice gobbler the first morning, which proved to be the only kill registered by hunters who belong to the cabin. I hunted fairly hard until late May when I went to British Columbia on a bear hunt. Nick Sabetto hunted with me several days. While we got close to birds, none were harvested as we usually made some sort of hunting mistake.

That fall I went on two elk hunts, one in Alberta and the other in New Mexico. I came home empty handed from Alberta, but did get a young bull elk in New Mexico. After returning from New Mexico in October, I came down with an illness that was never diagnosed and landed in the hospital for several days. Needless to say, I did not spend much time at the cabin. Several of the other guys did. While deer and turkeys were seen, nobody got either. The Dubbs family (Larry and Bill) hunted from the cabin with John and Chuck. Larry did manage to wound a doe that was unfortunately not recovered. This was the first time in quite awhile that neither game animal had been harvested from the cabin during the fall season.

2002: *Another "Sure Thing"*

During May, I hunted for several days, mostly on the big mountain. Having scouted frequently before the season opened, I had neither heard nor seen many turkeys, so hopes were not very high. John and Chuck once again decided to pursue turkeys elsewhere, leaving the cabin and surroundings to me.

The first morning I was located near my rock and, to my surprise, heard four different birds gobble. Unfortunately, I was unable to call any in for a shot. The one opportunity I had was a small jake that made a fatal mistake and came in silently, so I passed. Finally, on Wednesday of the first week, a jake with a five-inch beard presented too good an opportunity to pass up. I called the bird in twice. The second time, it stood on a log about twenty yards in front of me and gobbled. I couldn't resist the temptation. The balance of the season was spent trying to call in a bird for Nick Sabetto. There were several close calls, but no more birds harvested.

Archery season began later than it usually does this year, not starting until October 5. For some reason, nobody was in camp for the opener, which was highly unusual. Monday of the first week, I started hunting. Several deer were seen, including one buck on the first Friday (tending a scrape), but no shots presented themselves in the next few days.

Chuck joined me for the hunt on the second Saturday. I took a stand near my rock, and Chuck went to the edge of Terry Dennis's property. About 9:00, a doe and twin fawns passed me. I took the doe with a double lung shot at a distance of about thirty yards. For the morning, I saw six deer, one of which was a small buck. Chuck did not see any deer.

October 25, Bill Lloyd and his son Willy came to camp for the first youth early doe season. They were joined by Bill's brother Howie and his son Ian. Weather was cold and rainy with the temperature in the thirties and forties, but the boys were excited. That evening while hunting near my rock, Ian sighted a deer making its way down the mountain, which Howie took with one shot. Howie credited Ian with having seen the deer first and making it possible for him to kill it.

Rifle deer season was the coldest we had experienced since 1994. Bill, Howie, and their four sons were in camp with me. On the first day, all saw deer including bucks, but with the new antler restrictions in effect, nobody was sure enough that a buck was legal to take a shot. As usual, the other hunters had jobs or school to attend, so they went home that evening, leaving me alone in camp. On the second morning, Dave Hartman arrived, intending to hunt the rest of rifle season with me. Nobody else joined us, even on the two Saturdays, perhaps due to the brutal weather. We burned a huge amount of wood in the woodstove in order to keep the cabin warm. The temperature was 4° above zero when we left the cabin Tuesday morning. I went to my rock, and shortly before 8:00, a herd of deer worked their way past just downhill from me. One was a smaller buck, but not legal, so I picked out the biggest doe and took her with a neck shot from my .243. The doe weighed an estimated 140 pounds. This was to be the only kill from camp during the rifle deer season. Dave and I hunted hard for most of the two-week season and saw deer nearly every day, including several bucks.

Close to a foot of snow on Thursday of the first week made for interesting hunting, as it was really easy to see where the deer had been. The first Saturday, after returning to the cabin to warm up, I saw a legal buck from the back window. It had a spike on one side and a three-point antler on the other side. While it would have been legal for me to shoot it from the window of the cabin, I chose not to do so.

Muzzleloader season began with John, Chuck and Larry Dubbs hunting from the cabin. Several shots were taken, and Chuck wounded one doe, but it was not recovered.

2003: *One Tough Winter*

Winter continued to be one of the hardest we have had in recent memory, rivaling the one back in 1994. I didn't make it to the cabin nearly as often as usual during the winter, but it finally ended with a light snow as spring approached. I began scouting in earnest and heard several gobblers sounding off during early April. Some things had changed during the past year. Susie and Paul Smith, who inherited Albert Frehn's farm after he died the past year, had posted it, so that necessitated going there and asking for permission to hunt. As it is their land, I had no problem with that, but since I was the only one to ask for and get permission, we did not hunt there very much.

April 26 marked the opening of spring gobbler season. John, Chuck, and I were in camp. That morning, each of us saw gobblers. Chuck was first, seeing one early in the morning. It put on a bit of a show, but wouldn't come close enough for him to get a shot and finally made its way out of his area. I managed to call in three young jakes, but decided not to shoot a young bird so early in the season. John called in a nice mature gobbler and shot him at about twenty-five yards, but the bird got up, ran away, and was not found.

Nick Sabetto and I hunted one day the first week, but saw no birds. On the first Friday in May, I had some success, calling one young jake in so close that it almost stepped on me. A second larger gobbler hung up at a distance of over sixty yards. On Saturday, May 3, Chuck had the best chance, but the gobblers simply didn't want to talk to him. Late in the season, I finally dropped the hammer on a young jake and filled my tag.

Fall archery season began with John, Chuck, and me hunting from the camp. This season was quite different. An early muzzleloader season and a youth hunt provided a break in the six-week bow season. Chuck had one of the worst seasons ever. He did not see a single deer the entire archery season. John and I fared somewhat better, in that we saw more deer, including several nice bucks, but no game was harvested. I missed a buck during the first week, (underestimating the yardage) and saw a huge ten-point later in October (too far for a shot). The game commission's herd reduction program had been wildly successful. There were far fewer deer in the woods. What we hoped was that the antler restrictions imposed would give us larger bucks.

It was good to have youngsters in camp again. Bill Lloyd and his brother Howie brought three of their boys to camp during the early youth season and also several other times. These kids were already showing signs that they would be great hunters. Bill had finally made up his mind to leave his teaching job at Shippensburg for good (he thought). He was now a major in the Pennsylvania National Guard, and was teaching military science to ROTC students at Penn State. Hopefully, this could provide him more opportunities to hunt.

Rifle deer season opened December 1. My famous venison stew again graced the pot. (Perhaps this was the reason Chuck and John elected not to hunt out of the cabin.) Dave Hartman joined me on Sunday, and Bill brought his sons, Willy and Mike. Howie also showed up with his son, Ian. Dave recorded the only kill when he downed a doe mid-afternoon of the first day. Fewer deer were seen than on any prior opening of rifle season. This might have been due, at least in part, to the Grissingers and their gang driving the low ridge shortly after daybreak. Terry Dennis took a nice six-point early in the morning above his cabin. The Grissinger gang took three bucks on the first day, the largest being a ten-point. They also got an eight-point and a six-point.

Early Wednesday morning, I lucked into a raghorn buck with two broken antlers. I heard shots and got ready. When the buck appeared, I recorded my fifth buck kill at the rock. One of the broken antlers had the minimum required three points. I described the buck as "legal, but just barely." This was the first buck killed out of the cabin since 1999.

While not cabin related, I had several hunting adventures in other areas. Doris and I flew to the Republic of South Africa in March. I killed seven animals on this trip and nearly didn't survive a charge by a cape buffalo. In September, Larry Guise and I hunted in British Columbia. I harvested a moose and a mountain caribou. Larry got a nice caribou. Later in November, I took a beautiful mule deer in Idaho. I also finished my first book of hunting stories. One of the sections in the book is composed of stories about things that happened at Camp Bucktail.

The following three stories were published in my second book, THE LUCKIEST HUNTER IS STILL ALIVE, Llumina Press, 2008. Since I hold the copyright to that book, I am giving myself permission to reprint them here. Content wise, they are much better than what I had in the log book that was destroyed by fire, so they are included here with a few minor changes. Enjoy.

2004: A Pretty Good Year at Camp Bucktail

The 2004 rifle deer season was the climax of a pretty good year for those who hunt out of Camp Bucktail. It all started with archery season in October. For the first week, we hunted like we usually do, but saw few deer. We were seeing some nice bucks, however. I guess that is what antler restrictions and herd reduction will bring us.

I hunted nearly every day for most of the first two weeks of archery season, but didn't score. I was seeing deer, just not in huge numbers. One of the highlights of the first two weeks was a bear that wandered past my stand early one morning during the second week. A bear at ten feet gets the old heart pumping, let me tell you. This one was fairly large. I estimated his weight at nearly five hundred pounds. Not too long ago, seeing a bear in this part of the state was big news. It isn't now. Bears are everywhere.

On the first Saturday of early muzzleloader season, I decided to take my new inline for a walk. A herd of six does that I had been seeing on a more or less regular basis crossed in front of me, and I decided to take one of the mature ones. I had to wait until she cleared a blowdown, and when she did, I squeezed the trigger. After the smoke finally cleared, I walked over to examine her. It was a nice clean kill and a big doe with lots of meat for my son-in-law Crawford to make into his wonderful bologna, with a few steaks left over. As usual, nobody was around to help me drag my doe out. Our cabin lies in a hollow between Black Log Mountain and Lynne's Ridge. It doesn't matter where I shoot a deer. My drag is always downhill. Because of the distances I travel however, I sometimes have to drag my deer a mile or more. You have to go where they are to get them.

The early youth doe season brought Bill Lloyd, his brother Howie, and four of their sons to camp. Howie's son Ian hunted with his dad. His younger brother Cody was not yet twelve, so he could go along only as an observer. Will went out with his father. That left Mike, Will's younger brother, for me. I like taking youngsters out, so this was a treat for me. Mike is a typical twelve-year-old, full of energy and unable to sit still. After about two hours of waiting for deer to come by our stand, he decided that he would like to hunt the squirrels that were feasting on this year's abundant acorn crop. We walked back to the cabin and retrieved my old Savage .22. At the top of the ridge above camp, we encountered a few squirrels but did not harvest any. Mike wasn't familiar with my .22 and probably hurried his shots.

Bill had to leave camp at noon to get Will back to their home in State College for a parade, so we left the top of the ridge at 11:30. On our way down the logging road, a doe and two fawns came running toward us, obviously being chased off the big mountain by a hunter. The doe stood broadside to Mike at a distance of less than twenty yards. One of the fawns passed so close we could almost have touched him. Since we had left his .30-30 in camp to hunt squirrels, all we could do was wave at them. I guess we flunked Boy Scout motto on this one. We were not prepared.

The balance of archery season passed without major incident. I was seeing some nice bucks, but none came close enough for me to release an arrow. I saw one nice ten-point while hunting near a scrape he frequented, but he caught my scent when the wind changed, thus ending my best chance at him.

The first week of November, I usually spend most of my time hunting turkeys. For a change this year, I had booked a mule deer hunt in Montana, so I was gone for most of the prime turkey hunting. The beginning of November is also when most of the deer rutting activity takes place. When I left, the bucks were just starting to get crazy with the rut. A nice mule deer buck more than made up for the loss of Pennsylvania hunting time.

Finally, the first day of rifle season arrived. Dave Hartman joined me as my guest in camp for the third straight year. Bill and his two boys were there, but just to hunt the first day. Sunday evening, Bill and I decided that he would take Mike with him, and Will would go with me. I loaned Will my .257 Roberts to use, thinking he would enjoy shooting that rifle more than Bill's old .35 Remington which kicks like a mule. The old Roberts has a long history of being good deer medicine. I have taken close to thirty deer with it. It would do its job again this year.

We left the camp before daylight on Monday morning. Will and I hiked to the highest bench on Black Log Mountain, a trek of about forty-five minutes. On the way, we spooked a flock of roosting turkeys. The flock dispersed in perfect fashion, and I thought we might have fun calling some of them in later. Finally, we got to the bench, and I picked out a spot for us to sit where we could watch a draw leading to the top of the mountain. This place has yielded six whitetail bucks for me over the years, and I suspected it would be the perfect place for Will to take his first deer.

As the sky brightened, we could hear turkeys yelping. The flock was trying to get back together, so I thought I might help them a bit. I made a few yelps and clucks with my mouth call and immediately was answered by a lonely hen. Several of the lost birds came in fairly close, but when they saw our blaze orange outfits, they departed for parts unknown. By 8:30, most of the turkeys had left the area. Will and I kept watch for deer, knowing that soon, one would make its way into our area. Our patience was rewarded. Will spotted two deer moving downhill toward our position. His excitement level rose meteorically, but he kept himself in control. "One of them is a buck!" he told me. I responded, "Be patient. Wait until you have a clear shot." Time seemed to stand still until finally, the Roberts spoke.

Usually when I take a deer, it runs for some distance, but this one didn't. It simply disappeared. We waited about ten minutes, which was all the waiting Will could stand, and then walked over to the last place we had seen the deer. For a short time, we searched and then found the buck behind a blowdown less than twenty yards from where he had been standing when Will shot. As I approached him, I saw that he had a really decent rack with six points. I congratulated Will for making a fine shot.

Bill and Mike, having heard the shot and our shouts, arrived on the scene. I think Bill was more excited than Will. After all, this was the first buck ever taken by a member of the Lloyd family. Bill stated that he would get this one mounted. He and Mike then returned to their stand, and we field dressed the deer. Will and I began the chore of dragging him back to camp. The youngster was walking on air, so the drag wasn't as much of a chore as usual.

Back at Camp Bucktail, I hung the buck on our meat pole, but decided not to skin him until someone else returned to take photos of both of us with the deer. You want to remember your first buck, so I was determined to have a nice photo or two for us. Bill and Mike appeared later in the afternoon, and we took a whole bunch of pictures.

That evening when Dave returned from the mountain, he told of seeing a nice group of deer early in the morning. One was definitely a legal buck, but he couldn't get a shot at it. Perhaps it was one of the ten-points that our neighbor, Terry Dennis, had photographed with his trail camera. On his way back to camp, Dave stopped at Terry's cabin. Terry told him he took a nice nine-point that morning while hunting only a few hundred yards from his cabin.

Will Lloyd's first buck with his guide (me)

After the Lloyds left for State College with their buck, Dave and I settled into a routine that would last most of rifle season. We left camp early in the morning, hiked to our hunting spots, stayed all day, and returned to camp just before dark.

On Tuesday, I returned to the same place Will had taken his buck. During the day, I saw only two deer, but both of them were bucks. One was definitely legal, having two tines up off the main beam on both antlers, but he was a basket eight-point. I decided to let him pass. The other buck was a large spike with antlers over a foot long. He bedded down less than fifty yards away from me on the bench in full view. He stayed there for nearly an hour, and then walked away to feed. I count a day like this as a good day, since I would rather see one buck than ten does. Mid-morning on Tuesday, Dave killed a large doe high on the big mountain. He had a drag of almost a mile to bring it back to the cabin and spent most of the day butchering.

For Wednesday, rain was forecast. It came on schedule. Since Dave and I had most of the two weeks to hunt, we decided to take a day off and go home to do some chores. Dave had a masonry contracting business to run. He needed to check in with his guys and make sure things were running smoothly. I needed to replenish the wood and coal supply at the house so Doris and the mutts could stay warm.

Thursday through Saturday, Dave and I hunted hard, but didn't see anything we wanted to take. Deer came past our stands, just not the right ones. We covered a bunch of ground though. One thought came to mind. I saw only three other hunters after the first day. If guys weren't seeing deer, I suspect it was because they aren't spending time in the woods. Dave and I sure were.

We decided to give the deer a break on Monday of the second week. Tuesday, I hunted a stand on Lynne's Ridge, seeing a nice fat four-point and a doe. Wednesday, I promised Andy Grissinger that I would help him with his public sale. He decided he had enough of farming and sold the farm across Lynne's Ridge from our cabin. The sale went well for Andy. I hope he and Nora are happy in their new digs near Chambersburg.

Late Wednesday afternoon I got a chance to hunt Lynne's Ridge again. I did see two does, but no bucks this time. That evening Dave returned to hunt with me for the rest of the week. We plotted strategy and decided that we had given the big mountain enough rest. It was time to try the good spots near the top again.

We left the cabin Thursday morning before the flickers started flicking, or whatever it is that they do. The day was beginning to dawn as I reached the top bench and found my favorite rock, the scene of Will's first day success. I have done well over the years at this place, as previously mentioned, and decided to give it one more try. Not having slept well the night before, however, I soon began to doze. When this happens, the best thing to do is to take a short power nap, so I moved my backpack to a position behind me, leaned back, and went to sleep.

I must have been more tired than I thought, because when I finally awoke, it was 10:45. I shook my head to clear the cobwebs and sat up to survey the slope below me. Nothing was moving. I reached into my backpack and removed the thermos, pouring myself a cup of hot coffee. Things were good. God was in his heaven, I was hunting, and all was right with the world. Suddenly things got a bit more interesting.

A hundred yards below me and to my right, I saw movement. Deer! Buck! Antlers were visible. He had a Y that extended well above his ears.

My first thought was to let him pass, but after all, this was near the end of the second week of rifle season. A guy can be only so picky, so I took a closer look through my binoculars. The buck was walking with his head down in the manner of one that is looking for does. As he progressed southward along the slope, he stopped and turned his head. That is when I saw that he had brow tines. "Take him. He's legal," I thought to myself.

Slowly and carefully, I lowered the binoculars and picked up the old .257 Roberts. I raised it to my shoulder, centered the crosshairs behind the buck's shoulder, and squeezed the trigger. With the report, the buck kicked up his heels, ran a short distance, and then dropped, lying still about eighty yards from where I was sitting. The shot had been an easy one, the only one I heard all morning. Where were all the other hunters?

I put my rifle down and picked up my cup of coffee. While finishing it, I reflected on my luck so far this year. All things considered, this was a great year for deer hunting. The crowning achievement was Will's buck, for sure. This one was icing on the cake. He wasn't the biggest whitetail I have ever taken, but he was an adequate reward for my persistence. It goes to prove that if you spend enough time in the mountains, nice things do happen.

My second Thursday six-point

The drag back to camp was well over a mile, and by the time I got there shortly after 1:00, I was tired. It was a good kind of tired though. After hanging the deer, I skinned it and then washed the carcass out with lots of water. My butcher likes the condition my deer are in when I bring them to him. They are always clean enough to eat. After all, that is what we will do with the deer. I hate to see venison wasted. It is some of the best meat nature provides.

I took the carcass to the butcher shop that afternoon. When Dave returned that evening, we sawed the antlers from the head so I could mount them on a plaque later. Dave hadn't seen much that day, but this was the end of rifle season. Our deer had already received a PhD in hunter avoidance.

Friday and Saturday, I did a lot of walking in an attempt to push something to Dave. Finally, on Saturday morning, he filled his last tag with a nice doe. While we hadn't seen many deer this season, there were some nice bucks. The deer we took were in excellent condition, actually rolling in fat.

This 2004 season was the best we had so far in Camp Bucktail. We took more deer than ever before, while seeing fewer. I suspect the total weight of our deer was greater than that of any previous season. For sure, the bucks were better. A bunch of them were still out there. In the future, they will be smarter yet and a real challenge to kill. I hope I will be up to the challenge.

2005: Another Good Year at Camp Bucktail

This story begins a week before the 2005 rifle deer season opened when Larry Guise and Dave Hartman joined me for a day of hunting during Pennsylvania's bear season. Early Sunday morning, November 20, I traveled to camp and set about cooking some bear stew. On a British Columbia bear hunt in September, I killed a black bear and a grizzly and brought home a supply of meat from the black bear. This seemed to be an appropriate meal to serve for hunters who were hunting black bear.

Dave and Larry arrived in camp that afternoon. We went to the camp range and shot our rifles to make certain that sights were where we wanted them, and then I worked on the stew while we planned strategy. Following some considerable discussion and several bowls of the stew, which I must say was wonderful, we decided to hunt the top of the mountain above camp. That night we slept well, probably due to the amount of food in our bellies.

On Monday morning, November 21, we arose at 5:00 AM. Dave had butchered pigs the week before this, so he brought some of his scrapple to camp for our breakfast. While he fried the scrapple, I prepared a half-dozen sunny side up eggs and made toast.

With our guts properly stuffed, we left the cabin for the hard climb to the top of Black Log Mountain. It takes roughly an hour to negotiate this climb. Toward the top, the mountain becomes really steep. We took our time, stopping frequently to get breathing under control and avoid working up a rolling sweat. It was breaking daylight when we reached the summit. Dave worked his way around the point of the mountain. Larry and I went straight up to the top. When we got there, we were about a quarter of a mile from Dave. While there is always a possibility one of us might startle a bear, moving it toward the others, that didn't happen on this morning. We selected stands and settled in to watch the bench below us.

Although we didn't find any bears that day, all three of us did see a number of deer. Larry and I both got a look at a small herd of seven deer with a buck that was probably legal. Later in the morning I heard the groaning of a buck's tending grunt on the mountain above me. A doe emerged from the laurel, closely followed by a real wall-hanger of a buck. His antlers looked to be nearly twenty inches wide with a perfect ten-point configuration. Larry also saw this buck.

Dave and I took long walks later in the day, while Larry stayed put. Dave worked his way out the top of the mountain to the north, while I walked along the lower edge of the bench. By this method we hoped to move a bear so that one of us might get a shot. Again, this was not to be. When we returned to camp that evening, we felt good about our prospects for the coming rifle deer season. We had all seen quality bucks and enough deer to keep our interest. Now, the wait for rifle season would commence.

As usual, the hunters arrived on Sunday, November 27. Also, as usual, John hunted in the Bedford area. Chuck decided to hunt with a friend in the northeastern part of the state. Bill Lloyd and his two sons, Will and Mike showed up that afternoon. I cooked my world famous (for reasons yet to be determined) venison chili. I made a large twenty-quart pot of the stuff, enough to keep our bellies full for a few days. America needed the gas. While eating it, the guys used about half of a bottle of Texas Pete's hot sauce.

Dave Hartman got there about noon. As I mentioned previously, Dave does his own butchering. He brought more scrapple for breakfast and a few pork chops to break up the monotony of having chili for every meal. Dave ladled out the first bowl of chili and allowed as how it was satisfactory.

(Dave's ability to down food is legendary. On one fishing trip to Lake Ontario, Wayne Scubelek, Dave, and I all ordered twenty-two-ounce sirloin steaks. Wayne and I consumed about half of ours. Dave ate his, finished both of our steaks, and asked if I was going to finish my baked potato. Amazingly, he is also the thinnest of the group.)

During the afternoon, Bill Lloyd arrived in camp with his two sons, Will and Mike. Last year, Will hunted with me the first day and killed his first whitetail buck. This year it was Mike's turn to go with me. Mike had yet to take a deer of any kind, so he was more than anxious. Will, due to his success of the previous year, was now an old hand. I hoped to have the same sort of success with Mike this year, but I know full well that hunting is just that. If we killed a deer every day we hunted, we probably would call it shopping, not hunting. Mom had allowed the boys to take Tuesday off from school, so they would be here two days for a change. They were really looking forward to it.

The guys went to the rifle range in the hollow below the cabin and checked zeros on their guns. I had done this previously and knew that the two rifles I brought to camp were spot-on. They were my favorite Browning A-bolt hunter in .257 Roberts and my Weatherby Vanguard in .243 Winchester. The old Roberts is potent deer medicine. Both Will and I shot bucks with it the previous year. This year, Mike got the honor of using the Roberts. The .243 was a backup, just in case something went wrong with the Roberts. It never has, and it probably never will, but it pays to be prepared.

Sunday evening was a time for enjoying tall tales and the company of a bunch of hunters. In my opinion, there is nothing like that day in camp. You are anticipating a great day of hunting. Everyone is a successful hunter on the day before rifle season. The truth will be told the next day. Of course, it is difficult to get to sleep that night, but eventually the cabin rafters were rattling from the snores of sleeping hunters.

I don't need an alarm clock to get up before daybreak anymore. I arose to start breakfast. After turning on the coffee maker, I sliced the two-pound block of scrapple Dave brought, put some in the huge old skillet, and started it frying. Next, I cracked a dozen eggs into a mixing bowl, letting them sit until the scrapple was nearly done. For a larger number of hunters, it is much easier to do scrambled (I call them "strangled") eggs, so that was what I planned for this breakfast. Dave got up shortly after I did, and I put him in charge of making toast. A good-sized plate of strangled eggs, toast, and scrapple awaited each hunter, and soon they were digging in.

We left camp for the hike to our stands an hour before legal shooting time. Mike and I shouldered our backpacks and hiked up the mountain to the bench where Will took his six-point the first day last year. Bill and Will had a spot picked out a quarter of a mile from where Mike and I would be. Dave's favorite hunting haunt is close to the point of the ridge, nearly three quarters of a mile to the south of us. We all like to get high up on the mountain and away from the majority of hunters who don't go too far from the roads. It is safer there, and the deer know it. This day, however, the weather simply wasn't cooperating. The warm, foggy weather reduced visibility, and the woods were wet and quiet. Nothing moved, including the deer. We waited it out until nearly 1:30, and then Mike and I made our way back to the cabin to get some chili and check on the other guys. I tried to keep Mike's speed down to a slow trot, but it is impossible to hold a thirteen-year-old back. Sure enough, we jumped a pair of does who were hanging out in a thicket. These were the first two deer we saw.

When we arrived at the cabin, we saw a huge doe hanging from the meat pole. "Who got it?" Mike asked.

"I did," Will replied. "We saw it coming toward us, and I held the crosshairs on the sweet spot. The deer dropped right there." Dave later estimated that the doe would weigh in excess of one hundred fifty pounds. After skinning the doe, Dave took out the tenderloins and fish for our supper.

Since Will had a deer, Bill decided to take Mike with him that evening. I hiked to my rock which is located fifty yards uphill from the game lands property line. There is a bench along that line that the deer like to travel. This stand would be good to me again this rifle season.

As I was slowly walking back to camp on the old logging road, I saw four deer about fifty yards from me. I got my binoculars and gave them a good look, but none sported antlers, so I let them continue on their merry way. I had two antlerless deer tags in my possession, but didn't want to use them this early in the season. Maybe later in the week these ladies would be in danger, but not this particular evening.

Dave reported having seen the most deer. Early in the morning, he spotted a buck he was certain had legal headgear, but couldn't get a clear shot. He also saw eight does traveling together, but again was unable to put the crosshairs on one of the larger ones. While we had not seen as many deer as in years past, there were enough to keep us interested.

That evening, Dave took over the cooking chores. He prepared a feast of fresh deer tenderloin, boiled potatoes, and garden peas (Garden is what it said on the can). Nothing could have tasted better. Will was the proudest hunter in camp that evening. With bellies full, we skipped Monday Night Football and went to the racks to crank out some z's.

The weather comedian forecast horrible conditions for Tuesday. Heavy rain was being predicted for the afternoon. The morning brought fog in the higher elevations. The wind kicked up late that morning and limbs started to fall off trees. I didn't like that, so Mike and I made our way back to the cabin before noon. The sky opened up, and it started to pour shortly after we got there. We spent the afternoon in the cabin. About 3:00, Bill and the boys took off for their home in State College. They planned to stop at the butcher shop to drop off Will's deer. Dave and I settled in for the evening.

Dave and I usually hunt the entire rifle season. We burn a lot of firewood keeping the cabin warm. Dave is good company. We hunt different areas of the mountain, but keep in touch by cell phone at prearranged times for safety's sake. We hunted Wednesday and Thursday with very few sightings of deer. This is typical of our hunting. We usually don't see many deer where we hunt, but our chances of spotting a buck are good. Since I had not killed a deer this season, I decided to take a doe if the opportunity occurred.

On Friday morning, I hunted at a lower elevation for a change. I sat at a huge red oak tree downhill from the property line to the state game lands. This had been a good spot for me in the past. At 8:00, a herd of six does appeared. They were feeding their way across the oak flat below me. I picked out a nice one and put the crosshairs behind her shoulder. When I squeezed the trigger, she took off at a dead run, piling up less than fifty yards away. She would provide an ample supply of meat for the freezer, and I could now concentrate on getting my buck.

Saturday, Chuck Bailey showed up to hunt with us. On the first two days of the week, he hunted with some friends in northeastern Pennsylvania. He reported seeing a buck but had not been able to get a shot, so he was now here to try his luck in more familiar territory. I made the climb to my favorite rock above the oak flat. Chuck hunted to the northeast of me, and I thought he might move something past me. Dave, as usual, worked his way out to the southwestern end of the mountain. While we heard quite a few shots, none were close to us. I did see one red fox that had obviously been scared by something, as his motor was running at top speed.

That weekend brought us some frozen precipitation. A dusting of snow fell, followed by sleet. This made walking a bit noisier, a disadvantage to both hunter and prey. We hunted the high mountain on Monday again, finding numerous tracks and fresh deer droppings on top of the snow. Seeing no deer this day, I decided to check out the low ridge behind the cabin on Tuesday morning.

At the top of the ridge, I found a whole bunch of sign. Apparently, there was a herd of ten or more deer making this their home. While sneaking along the crest of the ridge toward the point, I caught a glimpse of several tails bouncing out ahead of me. Upon reaching the place where I had seen them, I found that the trails led down the hill. Obviously, the herd was heading across the road and up on the big mountain. It wasn't twenty minutes later that I heard Dave's .270 bark once, and then again.

Back at the cabin at lunchtime, Dave had a nice fat doe hung on the meat pole and was almost done skinning it. I helped him finish this chore and part out the deer for later butchering. Dave had a masonry job to do on Wednesday and Thursday, so he loaded his truck and went home. I decided to take Wednesday off and make certain my wife Doris had a sufficient supply of wood to keep the home fires burning. A major snowstorm was forecast for Thursday night, so this needed to be done.

I returned to the cabin Wednesday night after taking Doris out to dinner. Some might wonder why I was still hunting since my success had been limited to one doe so far. I love hunting. It is what I do with my free time, and since I am retired, I have a lot of free time. I love being in the outdoors. Seeing game is just a part of the process. Killing game is what happens when you are successful, but it isn't necessary to have had a great hunt. During a week in Manitoba in November, I saw twenty-three deer, but only two of them were decent sized bucks. I didn't drop the hammer on either one because I was holding out for a real boomer. I came home without a buck, but still enjoyed the hunt, even when it snowed all day and the temperatures were in the teens.

On Thursday morning, I got up as usual at 5:00. After switching on the pot of coffee, I heated water for instant oatmeal and toasted some bread. With an impending snowstorm, I figured the deer would be active this morning. They usually like to put away some groceries before a storm, and I thought that the oak flat below my favorite rock might be a good place to watch. I packed a lunch, ate my breakfast, and watched the channel ten news for about an hour. The weather forecast was worse, if anything. Up to eight inches of snow was expected for the overnight period. As the temperature was close to 10°, all of it would certainly be snow this time.

I left the cabin at 6:00 for the thirty-minute hike uphill to my rock. I have made this hike many times over the past eighteen years since we bought the cabin and can do it in total darkness. This is a good thing, because with the cloudy sky, it was very dark. The steepest part of the hike is the driveway leading uphill to Alleman's cabin across the road. Nobody hunts from this cabin after the first two days, so I didn't have to stop and say hello. I trudged on in the darkness, passing familiar landmarks along the way.

When I reached the base of the foot rocks, I took a short break and then hiked the remaining fifty yards uphill to my rock. At some time in the past, I constructed a seat out of flat rocks in front of this boulder. It is a comfortable place to sit and watch the oak flat below, which is an opening in otherwise dense forest along a main travel bench a few hundred yards below the summit of the mountain. Behind me, the rocks are filled with dense mountain laurel; the slope steep and rocky. To my right and left are thickets the deer feed and hide in. Immediately below, there is a clear view for some distance downhill along a logging road. I have taken a number of bucks and does from this vantage point, but I realized it was very late in the season. Still, like most hunters, I kept positive thoughts in my mind and was ready for whatever did or did not happen this day.

During the first hour, the woods were quiet. A few squirrels started to work the oak flat for the remaining acorns that a bountiful nature had supplied. One of the problems patterning deer this year stemmed from the abundance of acorns. They were everywhere, making a walk on the forest floor like walking on corn flakes, so the deer were extremely fat. At 7:30, a red fox worked his way near my stand, passing within thirty yards or so downhill. I wondered if he might have been the same one I saw on the first Saturday. He never noticed the blaze orange blob sitting motionless at the rock above him, and I wished I had brought my new digital camera. After the fox crossed into the thicket to my left, I settled back to continue my vigil. I broke out a granola bar, not particularly because I was hungry, but to ease the passage of time. Lunch was still four hours away.

Around 8:15, I noticed movement in the thicket downhill and to my right. "Deer!" I thought I saw a flash of antler, but wasn't sure. He was still nearly two hundred yards away and moving slowly along the bench. His path would take him across the opening in the woods about a hundred yards below me. I cranked the Leupold scope up to nine power and kept looking at him with my binoculars. When he broke into the open, I picked up the rifle and took my first look at him through the scope. I could clearly see that the antler toward me, his left side, had two points up off the main beam. He was a legal buck! I lowered the crosshairs to the sweet spot behind the shoulder and began the trigger squeeze that would end a beautiful animal's life.

At the report of the rifle, the buck leaped forward and ran at top speed for a short distance, disappearing into the brush. Resisting the urge to immediately follow him, I waited the required twenty minutes, and then picked up my things, shouldered my pack, and began the walk downhill. When I arrived at the spot I had last seen the buck, I found plenty of blood on the crust of snow and ice. It was an easy trail to follow, and shortly I spied the body of a deer lying against a tree. He was dead, having traveled slightly more than eighty yards from where I shot him. It had been a clean kill, and a decent eight-point buck did not have to suffer.

The chore of removing the entrails, bagging the liver and heart, and then moving the deer downhill to my cabin is a familiar one. First, I use my knife to cut a slit in the ear and tie my tag there with a piece of string. I then roll the ear around the tag and use the balance of the string to tie the ear tightly shut. This way I don't lose the tag on some stray bush or rock. I make my incision in the abdomen, opening the cavity to the base of the breastbone and rearward to the pelvis. Next, I reach inside the cavity to cut the diaphragm muscle lose from the chest wall, thus gaining access to the chest cavity. I reach upward as far as I can to cut the esophagus and windpipe. This releases the entrail package from the anterior end of the deer. After that, I lift the tail and cut around the anus, releasing the rectum from the body so I can pull it forward into the body cavity. (Some hunters like to split the pelvis to do this by banging on a knife with a rock. I like my knives too much, so I wait until I have the deer hanging on the meat pole and use a meat saw.) The last step is to remove the liver and heart from the entrail package and put them in a plastic bag I carry along for that purpose. Now comes the hard part, dragging the deer to the cabin.

Another second Thursday buck, this one an eight-point

When I got back to the cabin, I hung the buck for skinning. The sky was getting darker by the minute, so I finished as quickly as possible, removing the tenderloins and backstraps and placing them in bags so that I could process them when I got home later that afternoon. The rest of the carcass was dropped off at Grove's Butcher Shop in Saint Thomas to be ground into hamburger. We had enough steaks and roasts already in the freezer. I can't do that to backstraps and tenderloins, though. They are just too tasty as steaks.

The snow arrived as scheduled on Thursday night, dumping about eight inches of fluffy white stuff for me to plow on Friday morning. I got my tractor out to do our driveway. I also plow driveways for some of our neighbors. In return for the favor, they supply me with cookies. I think I am extremely well paid. After all, what are neighbors for?

When the plowing was done, I loaded my hunting gear into the Ford Ranger again and took off for the cabin. After a snowfall of this magnitude, the deer would surely be out feeding. I got to the cabin about half an hour before Dave and shoveled out the driveway so he could get his truck in. Next, I built a fire in the woodstove to warm the cabin. When Dave arrived, we got our gear ready and planned strategy. I decided to hike to the top of the low ridge, while Dave would set up an ambush for the deer at one of his favorite haunts on the high mountain. The theory held that, as happened before, my jaunt up on the low ridge might scare some deer into crossing the road and going up on the big mountain. But what happened on Thursday did not happen this day. Deer sign was everywhere on the top of the low ridge, though.

That night, we discussed at some length what we should do for the last day. We knew from the weather forecast that it would be cold. I decided to give my favorite rock stand one last try, as I couldn't think of a better place to go. Dave decided to hunt to my south again. We had a good night's sleep and arose fresh and rested, ready to go out and do battle again.

As usual, I made the hike past the cabin across the road and up the mountain into the foot rocks, getting to my rock shortly after 7:00. It was already daylight. I changed into heavy clothing, installed some foot warmers in my boots, and settled in. I didn't have to wait long.

At 7:30, I caught motion out of the corner of my eye. Three deer were making their way through the thicket to my left and approaching the open area. Their pace made it clear that something had startled them. I took a good look with my binoculars and felt sure that they were probably two does and one fawn of the year. I decided to take the first of the two does that presented a clear shot and picked up my rifle to be ready when they stepped out into the opening. When the first doe emerged, she did so in a bit of a hurry, so I never got the shot I wanted. The second one made a fatal mistake, however. She stopped to take a look around her in an opening, and I squeezed the trigger. She kicked up her heels at the shot and took off down the mountain. The other two kept moving at a rapid pace along the bench and in a more uphill direction. I got my things together and took out a cup of coffee to pass the twenty-minute obligatory wait. I experienced a feeling of sadness in knowing that I had no more tags left to fill. I took out my cell phone and dialed Dave's number to report my kill. When Dave answered, he sounded incredulous.

"You didn't!"

"Yeah, I did," I answered. I'll see you at the cabin.

"Do you need a hand dragging?" he asked.

"Nah. I think I can handle it, Dave. After all, this is the third time this season."

The drag to camp was, as usual, all downhill. I finished it and then hung the deer for skinning. This doe was rolling fat, just like all of the other deer we took this year. They definitely weren't lacking for food. The fat mass on her back was nearly an inch thick. I removed the tenderloins and backstraps. Since Dave had taken only one deer and my buddy Nick hadn't scored, I decided to let them have the rest of this one. I couldn't give up the loins and backstraps, though.

On Sunday, Nick stopped by the house and interrupted my football watching to thank me for thinking about him. Nick has had some real trouble with his shoulder and it required surgery. He was not able to get out as much as he wanted to this fall. Maybe the next year would be better. Nick is a good friend, and I hope to hunt with him again.

Our deer season at Camp Bucktail was the most successful ever. We took five deer during rifle season and one during the early muzzleloader season, bringing our total to six. While deer numbers are down from the high point of the late 1990's, the hunting is more rewarding to us. The deer were in great condition and achieving their genetic potential for growth. We were already looking forward to next year.

Muzzleloader addendum: December 27, by John Bartholow.

"Chuck, Larry, and I went to the cabin today to walk around. We played with a big flock of turkeys, probably forty birds in the bunch-all big adults. Chuck chased a bear up between Larry and me. He stopped about twelve steps beside me until he smelled me and took off. I smelled him on his way up the hill. Man, did he stink!"

2006: Yet Another Great Year

While the rifle deer and flintlock seasons of 2005 were cold, January of 2006 ushered in much milder weather than usual. Spring even came to us on time, more or less. April, the month when turkeys start to do their breeding, brought forth flowers right on schedule, and the gobblers gobbled on cue. High expectations were the norm for this turkey season.

Doris and I scheduled a hunting trip to New Zealand for the third week in April, and we came home with a full bag of memories. I took three great animals, the best of which turned out to be a world class fallow deer. A few weeks later, I departed for a bear hunt in Alberta with my old friend, Lenny Gransch. Two other hunters, Wayne Scubelek and Brad Bard, went along. All three of us took great black bears. This year was starting out great for me.

Spring gobbler season typically has some incidents that are noteworthy. Even though I hunted a lot less this one than others, it was no exception. On one occasion while calling turkeys, a grey fox came within ten feet of me. On another, I called a gobbler in and had him work his way to a spot only a few feet behind me. I never got a shot at him. One more gobbler came in silently, got fairly close, and gobbled so loud that it startled me, thus ending the game when I moved. John Bartholow, as usual, had several close encounters of the feathered kind, but did not score either.

During August, I went to Alaska on my first sheep hunt. This one didn't turn out so well. Not all of them end up the way you want them to. My Wyoming elk hunt in September turned out a whole lot better. Doris and I had a wonderful time, and I took a nice six by six bull elk. We brought the meat home with us, so this removed the pressure of having to fill the freezer with deer meat this year.

September scouting trips at the cabin brought mixed results. I did see a number of good bucks and got video footage of some does and fawns, but the deer count was way down compared to previous years. I didn't hunt as much with the bow this year, and nobody got a deer during the early muzzleloader season either. I took Cody Ferrell, a twelve-year-old neighbor, hunting for his first time in October's youth squirrel season, and he harvested his first bushytail. A new hunter was born.

Turkey season came in October 26. John Bartholow and Chuck Bailey joined me at the cabin for the first day. Chuck, a high school shop teacher, was recovering from an accident in school and couldn't use his shotgun. He borrowed a .222 from John and ended up taking a nice bird with it.

Dave Hartman got a bird on Monday of the following week, his first since he began hunting at Camp Bucktail. It took me until Friday of the second week to get a bird. As is typical, it was one of those things that don't work out exactly as expected.

I went to the cabin on Wednesday night, planning to hunt with the bow Thursday morning. It is nice to overnight at the cabin because I can get up later, have a good breakfast, and then hike up into the mountain to hunt without having to drive half an hour. The hike to my rock brought a sweat to the brow. I settled in to my seat and almost immediately heard a turkey gobble on the high bench above me. After putting a call in my mouth and giving a few yelps, I heard birds making their way down the hill toward me. I put down my bow and picked up the video camera to take some footage, figuring that the birds would not give me any chance with the bow. I got some wonderful shots, but suddenly realized that the birds were in bow range. Slowly, I put down the camera and picked up the bow, only to hear those dreaded alarm putts. As the birds moved away from me, I took a shot at approximately twenty-five yards, but missed. There went my chance to harvest a mature gobbler with the bow.

After lunch, I decided that if the mountain wanted to give me turkeys, I would take the shotgun for the evening hunt. The reader has probably guessed how this one turned out. Close to quitting time, a nice eight-point, neck swollen by the rut, walked past my stand less than twenty yards away. This would have been a fairly easy shot because he stopped when I grunted, standing broadside with a clear shot to the vitals. As it was, he got to look for girlfriends for another day.

The next morning, deciding that since I was always armed with the wrong weapon, I would just give up and go squirrel hunting. Instead of the bow or shotgun, I took my .22 rifle along with me to the high bench. Squirrels were everywhere. Within half an hour, I had two tree rats lying dead at the base of an oak tree. I was getting ready to retrieve them when I noticed movement. A flock of turkeys made its way uphill about a hundred yards from me. When a grey fox made a rush at them, they all flushed, going in different directions. One of the birds flew directly toward me and landed only ten yards away. I took a bead on its head and had

Thanksgiving dinner flopping in front of me. This was a great morning of hunting. I had two squirrels for my neighbor Willy Cuff and a turkey for Doris. Sometimes Diana, the goddess of the hunt, smiles on a hunter. This was my day for a smile.

I took Cody hunting one more time. He shot half a box of shells but didn't hit even one squirrel. Next year he will be a better shot, I hope. What he lacks in shooting skill, he makes up for with enthusiasm.

Crawford and I went to Ohio the third weekend in November. We hunted with an outfitter that had been in business only two years. Crawford got a nice eight-point that I scored at one hundred fourteen inches by the SCI measuring system. We had such a good hunt that we booked for the last week of October, 2007. This would take place during Ohio's archery season. Larry Guise, another friend who had begun to hunt with me, and Crawford's father would join us. We were looking forward to it.

The following week, I helped Crawford and his father make some wonderful deer bologna. We spent four hours grinding and stuffing until we had over sixty pounds worth, which provided some great snacking throughout the following year.

The three-day bear season opened, as usual, the Monday before Thanksgiving. I had to hunt by myself. Dave usually hunts with me, but this year he went to Tennessee for a visit with family. Larry Guise elected to hunt with another friend in Mifflin County.

What a bear season! This was maybe the best ever, at least so far, because I actually saw bears. I started hunting bears way back in the 1950's when I was twelve years old. Of course, in all of those years, I had yet to take one in Pennsylvania.

Sunday evening, November 19, I left my warm abode in Saint Thomas for camp. The cabin has a few creature comforts, like electricity and a wood burning stove, but no flush toilet. Horrors! We added satellite television a few years back so the members could enjoy Saturday football. I settled in to a routine that makes such trips worthwhile. Dinner consisted of venison tenderloin, potatoes, and canned green beans. I then popped the cap on a foamer and kicked back to enjoy solitude. After watching a quarter or so of the football game, a good night's sleep seemed more important, so I hit the sack.

On Monday morning, I arose at the ungodly hour of 4:30 AM. After a sausage and egg breakfast, I loaded my backpack with nearly everything I like to take along for a day afield. The kitchen sink won't fit. This included two peanut butter sandwiches, some fruit and grain granola bars, and a thermos of coffee that was strong enough to walk but not yet old enough to vote. I also took spare shells for my .30-06 rifle. About fifteen minutes before it got light, I shouldered my pack and rifle and departed the cabin for the half-mile walk to the high bench.

Along the way, I jumped a doe and a buck that were doing doe and buck things. The buck was one of the best I have seen this year, but it was too dark to determine whether he was the ten-point I saw earlier. I made my way uphill, working up a sweat during the process. At my age, working up a sweat is easier to do than it was twenty years ago. I reached the last bench before the top of the mountain and sat down to watch the oak flat below. The temperature being near freezing, I made myself as comfortable and warm as possible.

About 7:30, hearing a twig snap behind me, I turned slowly to see what had made the noise. "Buck! A four-point!" As the youngster made his way along the bench behind me, he finally caught a whiff of something that didn't belong in his woods and departed at a trot. Half an hour later, a second buck appeared, coming from the same direction. This time I was watching and caught movement. I raised my binoculars and was able to count four points on each side. This buck was clearly not a mature buck like the one I saw before daybreak. His antlers were thin, but he showed promise of being a real wall-hanger if he managed to avoid hunters like me for another year or two. He worked his way downhill below me and continued on his way, totally unaware of how close his brush with death had been. Deer season was a week away, and he had been in no danger this morning. Another hour passed with only the antics of squirrels and the occasional yelp of a turkey to add some interest to the day. Things would soon get a tad more exciting, however.

Shortly after 10:00, I caught movement downhill and to my right. "A bear!" I raised my rifle slowly and carefully, disengaged the safety, and prepared to shoot when I got the chance. "Wait a minute! A second one?"

Now there were two black objects moving on a course that would take them right below me on the bench. It was a mother bear and her cub of the year. I estimated that the cub would weigh about seventy pounds or so. Momma was considerably larger. Either would be legal game, so I had to decide whether to shoot or let them pass. Personally, I dislike shooting females with cubs, so the decision was an easy one. Let me stress that this was a personal decision, and I would hold nothing against anyone who decided differently. I put the rifle back on safety. Momma and her progeny were feeding on the plentiful acorns and appeared to be rolling fat, hibernation being just a few days away for them. They fed on without knowing I was there.

The rest of the day passed uneventfully. I did see a few more deer and a multitude of squirrels and chipmunks. The evening walk back to the cabin is all downhill and considerably more pleasant than the morning one. I had spent a day afield without getting anything. Most days of hunting are like that. You spend a whole lot of time hunting and not much time killing. That is good enough for me.

On Tuesday morning, I decided to check out another area of the mountain. The climb to the high bench again brought out a sweat. While standing on my coat, I stripped off the sweaty layers of clothing, changed into dry clothing, and added a wool sweater. The air always seems cleaner near the top of Black Log Mountain than it is anywhere else in the world. Maybe that is just my perception. I settled down to wait and see what might appear this morning. Perhaps that lonely boar bear would decide to put in an appearance.

At 7:45, the solitude was interrupted. My eyes detected motion lower on the slope below me. Four deer were making their way upward toward the top of the mountain. All of them were of the antlerless variety, one a button buck, as evidenced by the dark brown patches in front of his ears. I let them pass, unaware of my presence. One of the older does kept looking back where they had come from. I have seen this behavior before. It usually means that a buck is following. I concentrated on the slope below the group of deer. Shortly, another larger deer appeared. This one sported antlers. I looked through the binoculars and could count four points on one side of his rack with three on the other. He too passed by, oblivious to my presence. I filed this information away for future use. This might be a place to bring one of Bill Lloyd's sons to hunt next week on the first day of rifle season. While I would certainly take this seven-point buck myself, I derive more enjoyment from seeing a youngster kill his first deer, and Mike Lloyd had yet to get one.

At noon, I decided it was time for lunch. I removed the lunch bag and bottle of water from my pack and took out one of the two ham and Swiss cheese sandwiches. As I was munching on the sandwich, a pileated woodpecker landed in a tree above me and began drilling for his lunch. The pileated woodpecker is the largest of the Pennsylvania woodpeckers, about the size of a crow. He sports a red head with a crest and has some white on his wings. His drilling showered the forest floor with wood chips. Eventually he flew on to the next tree, and I was left to finish my lunch without the jackhammer racket of Mr. Pileated.

Later in the afternoon, I spied motion on the mountainside below me. Something black was working its way through the brush patch. I hoped for a bear, but was only a little disappointed when it turned out to be a small flock of turkeys. They spotted my blaze orange and were quickly gone from the area. Nothing much happened the rest of the afternoon, save the visits by squirrels and chipmunks. At sunset, I made my way downhill to the cabin, thinking that this just might have been the best bear season ever, and I didn't even fire the gun.

Rifle season came in with a bang. On the first day, I took a doe from a herd of six that came to my stand. Will Lloyd got a shot at one of them, but missed. On the second day, Dave Hartman scored on a doe. That was the total of our kill for rifle season at Camp Bucktail. Dave and I hunted hard for the rest of the two weeks and saw a few bucks, but we were never sure that they were legal, so we let them walk.

John got a nice eight-point during rifle season while hunting with his buddy Maynard near Bedford. He brought the antlers to the cabin later on for us to see. Since I am now an official measurer for Safari Club International, I volunteered to measure the antlers for him. It scored just over one hundred, a pretty nice Pennsylvania buck.

I did have a tag for another wildlife management unit, so on Wednesday of the second week, Nick Sabetto and I went there to hunt. For quite a number of years, our group hunted in Black Log Valley, Juniata County. This valley is located about thirty miles from Camp Bucktail. We used to drive out a road along a big bench, but in recent years the state had closed the road to motor vehicle traffic. Nick and I climbed the mountain and hunted there for most of the day, but didn't see any deer. There was lots of sign, however. Maybe this would be a place to keep in mind for future seasons. It has always been a pleasure to hunt with Nick. He truly is one of the good guys.

Flintlock season is a fun time to be in the woods, and this one was no exception. John and Larry Dubbs, along with Larry's son Bill, hunted a number of days at the cabin during this season. I joined them several times. We saw deer nearly every time we hunted, but nobody scored. Primitive weapons season presents special challenges. I did have a chance on the next to last day when a doe and fawn passed only fifty yards or so from me, but decided not to drop the hammer. They would be here next year. Besides, the freezer was full of meat.

WINTER INVENTORY

This story appeared in my first book, THE LUCKIEST HUNTER ALIVE.

It snowed February 11, 2006, so two days later I went for a walk on the mountain above our cabin. After a fresh snowfall, I like to check for tracks made by those deer that nobody thinks exist. At least that is what most of the "hunters" I talk to seem to be saying lately. Of course, I didn't see any of those "hunters" up high where I hang out during hunting season.

It was 8:30 before I left our cabin. The hike uphill had me nice and warm by the time I got to Carl Alleman's cabin. Carl's brother Ray used to hunt there, but this year nobody from their group hunted during rifle season. I wonder why. This area has produced a number of bucks and good tasting does for me in the eighteen years several of us have owned Camp Bucktail. It helps keep us supplied with meat. I love it here.

I worked my way up the logging road above Carl's cabin. Trudging up the mountain, I crossed the tracks of five or six deer that had fed along the first bench. They pawed up a wide area in search of acorns, obviously finding some leftover from fall. I continued uphill toward my favorite rock where I had fashioned a seat out of two flat rocks in front of this huge boulder. It is my best stand during rifle season. So far, I have taken six bucks from this stand alone. Each of the last two years I have killed a nice buck on the second Thursday of rifle season. Last year it was a prime eight-point. The tracks of several deer showed they passed just a few yards below my seat.

I turned to the north, walking along the state game lands property line, and crossed a set of three tracks. Farther on there was a single set. This deer dragged his toes on the snow. "Probably a buck," I thought. Bucks do that stiff legged trot and drag their feet when they travel. The size of his hoof prints indicated a large animal. At least one buck is left for next year.

Coming down off the mountain, I crossed the hard road and then hiked to the top of Lynne's Ridge. On the bench near the top, the trails of several deer made their way along the flat, heading toward the oak stand near the end of the ridge. The bumper crop of acorns we had this fall would feed them for some time. A short distance uphill from the deer tracks, I cut the trail of a coyote. He was on a hunting trip too, looking for breakfast. This is the mean season for wildlife in our woods. They must live off the stored fat from summer and fall, and they slow their systems down to conserve energy. I hiked onward to the top of the ridge.

A logging road goes down the middle of the spine on Lynne's Ridge. I walked toward the south end. It simply amazed me how many sets of deer tracks I crossed. My best guess is that at least twenty deer call this ridge their home. The deer feed in the farm fields below. One huge field is a mixed hay field. They seem to love the stuff. Two fields of corn were planted along the creek. The buck I took on the mountain last December had a paunch full of corn.

Back at the cabin, I poured myself a cup of hot coffee and sat for awhile to reflect on what I had seen this morning. Things are better as regards the deer population than some hunters seem to think. However, we may never again see the time when fifty deer cross our paths in one day. We need to adapt to the new situation. I guess some might give it up. It will be their loss, not mine. I can't wait until it snows again. I need more mornings like this.

2007: *The Beginning Of The End*

During January of 2007, I saw an advertisement on the huntingpa message board for a hunting camp in Somerset County. The camp included a log cabin and twenty acres of land. After Crawford and I journeyed out to take a look at it, we decided to purchase it. This became the beginning of the end of my hunting at Camp Bucktail. One thing you can't take away from me would be the many memories of good times had there. It was a part of my life, one of the two most favorite places in my heart and will remain so forever. Time marches on and things change. More on this new camp would follow.

While we hunted fairly hard during spring gobbler season, no birds were taken. Some days it was hard to find them. Perhaps this was due to a really wet and cold nesting season the previous year. This year seemed to be better, so we had something good to look forward to next fall.

Autumn arrived and hunting season began as usual with archery season. Crawford and I were travelling to our new hunting camp in Somerset County, so I spent less time at Camp Bucktail. I took a doe on the second Saturday of archery season at the new camp with my crossbow. This would turn out to be the last season I hunted very much out of Camp Bucktail.

The Lloyds (Bill, Mike, and Will), Cody Ferrell (a neighbor boy from Saint Thomas), and I did hunt a few days during early muzzleloader season the third week of October. Bill had the first Camp Bucktail kill of the year, taking a doe while hunting on top of Lynne's Ridge. Dave Hartman joined the group on Saturday, October 20. Using my inline, he took a nice doe off the top of the mountain. Deer seemed to be less numerous than in other years, but there were still enough that we all encountered some.

Fall turkey season came in. John harvested a bird on November 6 in Bedford County, but no kills were recorded at the cabin.

Rifle deer season found the Lloyds in camp, with Will's friend Tyler Smith also there. John Bartholow killed a nice eight-point buck in Bedford County on the first day. Will and Tyler both took does on the second day. While hunting at my rock on the last day of the season, Chuck harvested a doe.

I took a young buck that had shed his antlers with the flintlock while hunting with Chuck, John, and Larry Dubbs on December 28. This brought the total number of deer taken while hunting out of Camp Bucktail this year to six, the highest total ever. (It should be noted that this year was long after the big reduction in the deer herd took place.)

Log of Game Taken at Camp Bucktail

1987 – Pat and George-turkeys
1988 – John-twin turkeys
George-doe – flintlock
1989 – George, Crawford Peters, and Jack Stayer-turkeys
Chuck – five-point – first buck killed at the cabin
George and Crawford-does
1990 – John and Crawford-turkeys
Crawford – six-point
Pat – three-point
1991 – Pat and George-turkeys
Chuck – three-point (unicorn)
George – six-point
1992 – George – four-point
1993 – Chuck-doe – archery(first cabin bow kill)
George-doe – rifle
Pat-doe – flintlock
1994 – George-doe – archery
John-gobbler
1995 – George- eight-point
1996 – Chuck, John, and George-fall turkeys
George-button buck (doe season)
1997 – George-fall turkey and spring gobbler
George-doe – archery
Bill-doe
1998 – George – three-point
1999 – George-doe (archery) and spike buck (rifle)
Larry Dubbs-fall turkey and doe – flintlock
Bill-doe

2000 – George- spring gobbler

Chuck-doe – archery

Bill-doe

George-two does – archery

2001 – Chuck-spring gobbler

2002 – George-spring gobbler

George-doe with bow

Howie Lloyd-doe – early season

George-doe – rifle season

2003 – George-spring gobbler

Dave Hartman–doe – first day of rifle season

George–doe and "legal" buck – rifle season

2004 – George–doe – early muzzleloader season

John-turkey – first day of fall turkey season

Will Lloyd-six-point-first day of rifle season (Will's first deer)

Dave Hartman-doe-second day of rifle season

George-six-point-Thursday, December 9

2005 – Will Lloyd-doe-first day of rifle deer season

George – doe – first Friday

George – eight-point – second Thursday

George – doe – last Saturday

Dave Hartman – doe – Monday of the second week

Bill Lloyd-four-point

2006 – Chuck Bailey-hen turkey – first day of fall turkey season

Dave Hartman-hen turkey – October 31

George-hen turkey – November 10

George-doe – rifle season

Dave-doe – rifle season

2007 – Bill Lloyd-doe-early rifle season

Dave Hartman- doe-early muzzleloader season

John – 8-point -rifle season – Bedford County

Will Lloyd – doe -rifle season

Tyler Smith – doe -rifle season

Chuck Bailey – doe -rifle season

George -antlerless buck-December 28 – flintlock season

2008 –   Larry Dubbs – spring gobbler

George- spring gobbler

Will Lloyd- five-point

2010 –   Bill Lloyd – five-point – first day – Bill's first buck

23 year totals (since 1987):

bucks-18

does-35

turkeys-27

Following the spring of 2007, I did not hunt very much out of Camp Bucktail. Most of my hunting time was spent at our new camp in Somerset County. Tragedy struck during the 2012 hunting season when Mike Lloyd and a buddy were in camp. They left the cabin to go hunting on the big mountain, and the wood burner must have overheated, setting the camp on fire. It was a total loss. That spring and summer we cleaned up the site and made arrangements to purchase a shed/cabin shell from North Mountain Structures in Edenville near our home in Saint Thomas. We hired an excavator to do the site preparation. Along the way, I decided it was time to sell my share, and the other guys bought me out. This ended my association with Camp Bucktail.

The guys did rebuild. They purchased that 14 X 40 prebuilt cabin shell and finished the interior. Doris and I visited the new camp to see how it turned out. It is really much nicer than the old green cabin. I wish them lots of good times.

What was left of Camp Bucktail after the fire

SECTION II

A New Beginning: The Camp Rip-N-Tear Story

2007: A New Beginning

Being an avid hunter, I try to stay up on happenings in my area of interest. While checking on huntingpa.com one cold January day, a website I used to frequent, an advertisement for the sale of a cabin situated on twenty acres in Somerset County came to my attention. Out of curiosity and mentioning it to my son-in-law, Crawford Peters, who lives over the mountain in McConnellsburg, we decided to check on it. I called the owner who resides in Bedford, Steven Sabo, and he informed us as to how he was running an online private auction that would end on a Sunday in mid-April. Arrangements were made to visit the cabin. Crawford and I drove west through Somerset and then headed southwest about twenty-five miles to a small rural town called Confluence, named for two joining rivers (the Youghiogheny and the Casselman) and a creek (Laurel Hill Creek) that come together there. We turned north on Draketown Road and traveled about two miles. Turning left on a narrow road named Back Road, we passed a few houses and cabins. The paved road changed to gravel but was still easy driving. For the most part, we were in a wooded area. We found the pipe gate at the opening to the driveway and traveled about a quarter mile uphill to the cabin which could not be seen from the road.

There it was! The cabin, a two-story rustic log structure looking much as we dreamed a camp would look, sat in a clearing with large trees all around it. To the left was a barn/shed type building with a lean-to in front that could be used for storage. We knocked on the door, and it was answered by Mr. Sabo. He told us that he had another couple inside who were also interested, and if we would like to take a walk and explore the area for half an hour, he would appreciate it. We agreed and set off on a walkabout. A trail across the driveway from the cabin took us downhill to a small stream named Glade Run. An old road led into state game lands #111 with over ten thousand acres bordering the property. The camp driveway actually had been part of this road. Originally it led to a homestead, the foundation of which is still there. We found later that this road is Harbaugh Road, named after the homesteader whose home was near an old field in the game lands half a mile from the cabin. The twenty acres of land on which the cabin sat was all forested. I identified white, red, and pin oak trees among them, indicating an acorn crop could be a game magnet.

The cabin on a very unusual January day with no snow

The inside had just about everything we would need, including a good kitchen, living room, bathroom, and a large bunkroom upstairs to house several hunters comfortably. Electricity and water were there, two pluses. No septic system was present, but an electric (incinerating) toilet was installed. No phone line was in evidence, and we discovered that cell phone service was spotty. A television sat on a small table in the living room. It was connected to an outside aerial and had very snowy reception. These were minor inconveniences. Crawford and I decided that we really wanted this cabin, so we entered the bidding war.

At this point, we were told some other bidders also had been looking at it. Not all of them were interested in a hunting cabin. Some just wanted a recreational place. Being a hunter himself, Mr. Sabo seemed to be rooting for us. I kept checking on the bidding, increasing our bid when necessary, and hoping it did not go beyond what we could pay. At last, in mid-April, the day came, and we were told we were the high bidders. After three months of hoping, we were thrilled beyond belief. Settlement was scheduled for May 23, but prior to that, Mr. Sabo gave Crawford a set of keys and permission for us to use the camp. Upon exchange of large sums of money and signing papers on settlement date, we became the official owners of our camp.

Some old friends joined me in hunting at the new camp. Dave Hartman would be indispensable, with his strong back providing much of the hard stuff that has to be done on occasion. (In fact, he is the subject of a story about how much he contributes in another book I am working on.) The reader has also met Larry Guise in some of my previous efforts. Larry hunted on occasion with us at Camp Bucktail and is still one of the toughest people I know. He has several health issues and puts up with lots of physical discomfort. Nick Sabetto showed up from time to time. Nick is good company. Some new neighbors would be introduced in future segments of this story, including relatives of Mr. Sabo who owned properties adjoining the camp. His son Craig owned the tract to the south, and son Richard owned the tract immediately north of ours, plus two acres between our tract and the state game lands. We would later buy that smaller tract from him, bringing our total acreage to twenty-two. One of their cousins, Rick Steinmiller, owned a camp along Back Road just a quarter mile east of this cabin. Over the coming years we would become friends with Mr. Steinmiller and some other camp owners on Back Road. Scott Hamilton owned a camp across back road from our driveway, and we got to know him as well. In later years, we would also get to know Joe and Mark Giovannitti and Gerry Timcik, some other Back Road camp owners.

While this cabin had most of the essentials for a hunting camp, there were a few drawbacks. One of them was the lack of a proper sewage system which would be inconvenient, but in my mind, not insurmountable. When, in the future, we decided to get a permit for a sand mound system, we discovered that Mr. Sabo had managed to alienate the Lower Turkeyfoot Township officials to the point that obtaining such a permit became a major undertaking. We also discovered that the township prohibited temporary toilets and holding tanks (known as jiffy johns or job johnnies) such as what we used at Camp Bucktail. We bought one anyway and put it in one side of the shed that came with the cabin so it would be out of sight. Just as it had been at old Camp Bucktail, the morning constitutional during winter was an adventure in discomfort. Nobody ever wanted to be the first to warm the seat.

At some point that spring or early summer, a name for our new camp was decided upon. Way back in the 1960s, Doris and I had raised and trained English setters for hunting and field trials. Our kennel name was RIPPANTARE. We campaigned our setters in horseback shooting dog competition as the Rippantare Setters. For some reason, when Crawford decided to start a business repairing motorcycles and actually building a few from scratch, he named the business Rip-N-Tear Customs. The similarity to our old kennel name was fine with me. Crawford's father later made us a sign with our camp's name to post over the door.

Summer of 2007 was spent doing chores such as changing locks and getting the camp set up the way we wanted it. Mr. Sabo included some essential furniture with the cabin, including a recliner, a sofa, a large dining room table, and several beds in the bunkroom upstairs. We added to that from our homes and additional purchases making the cabin a comfortable place to spend time. Crawford constructed a tripod supported feeder in his home workshop, and we put it out close to the cabin. The feeder consisted of a large galvanized garbage can with a timed feed dispenser that spun out a portion of corn morning and evening. Some nice bucks and does showed up to eat the corn it dispensed. One morning while Dave and I were in camp, a group of bucks came in to the feeder together. We decided to invest in trail/game cameras. Over the ensuing years we got outstanding photos of game animals including deer, bears, and turkeys.

During the next few months, I made a number of trips to our new camp. Usually I was by myself, but on some trips Crawford, Dave, or Larry came along. Crawford had a business to run, Dave had a masonry job, and only Larry was retired like me. Our efforts were directed toward scouting the area to find out where to hunt. We found three wooden stands close to our camp. Two of them were on Craig Sabo's tract, and one was on Richard Sabo's two-acre tract. Deer sign seemed to be sparse with no easily discerned patterns. A few game trails were discovered, but none appeared to be heavily used. Local hunters I talked to complained that the Pennsylvania Game Commission's herd reduction program had gone way too far, but what we were seeing in the photos taken by our game cameras seemed to indicate a fairly healthy population of deer. Time would tell which of these contrasting views was true.

October finally arrived bringing with it the archery deer season. Obviously, this was highly anticipated, so several of us did the hunting thing. I ventured out to camp with Larry Guise that first week, but while we spent a lot of time hunting, neither of us saw many deer. Larry had to go home on Friday. Crawford and his dad joined me in camp for the weekend. On Saturday morning, I climbed into a ladder stand I had placed along the hollow to the east of camp, a short distance uphill from Back Road. As the morning went on, I heard a door slam at Scott Hamilton's cabin, and a conversation could be heard taking place there. Within a minute, a herd of six does and one basket eight-point buck materialized, travelling at a quick walk. As they came past me, I raised the crossbow and got ready to take a shot at the buck when one became available. I did not have a great shot at him, so I changed my aim and took one of the does instead. When I squeezed the trigger, I could see the arrow enter her chest. She ran toward the camp driveway and collapsed on the other side of it. This was our first camp kill and the first animal taken with my new crossbow. When Crawford and his dad returned for lunch, I already had the doe skinned, quartered, and on ice in the cooler. While all of us hunted hard, that was the extent of our success for this early season.

Our first hunting season at camp was certainly a learning experience. During October, Larry Guise joined me in camp. Most of the time, Dave was working. He showed up when he could get some time off from his job. The temperature one morning hovered in the freezing range with a dusting of snow, and Larry observed, "Oh, my! I don't have clothes for this." We quickly learned that Somerset County is a different world. Snow and cold temperatures can come any time of the year. We didn't see many deer, but the more time we spent in the woods, the more sign we found, indicating that they were around here. There also appeared to be a decent population of turkeys and bears, as evidenced by the abundant sign.

Crawford, with his doe from greenbriar hell

On the first day of rifle deer season, Dave and I went past the game lands fields to hunt the oak flat and an area west of it that we soon called greenbriar hell. This tangled mess, located above an oak flat roughly three quarters of a mile from camp, was a real challenge to walk through. Both of us saw bucks. One of the two I sighted was an eight-point, but I never got a clear shot at him. That is how hunting goes sometimes. Larry hunted out of a stand close to Back Road, hoping for hunters to push a buck out of the farm fields, which did not happen. Crawford and Nick Sabetto joined us the second day. We hunted the two weeks of rifle season with the hunting group's composition changing from time to time.

During the first week, Dave hunted a good bit of the time in green briar hell. He had seen deer there on a regular basis, so when Crawford decided he wanted a doe for the freezer, Dave sent him there. He had been sitting for less than an hour when one came by, so we ended up with a total of two does to show for our efforts this season. One thing we did learn was that snow can come anytime from October on, and you had better have warm clothes with you when it does.

2008: *Exploring New Territory*

Winter brought us plenty of snow, but eventually spring came around that corner, wherever that corner was at the time. I made a number of trips to the new camp with the objective being to do winter inventory. During January and February, the ground was consistently covered with snow, and at times it got deep. That photo at the beginning of this section showing the cabin in January of 2007 with no snow on the ground proved to be an exception. On most January days, there would be lots of the white stuff.

Tracks in the snow do not lie, and there were plenty of them. On one of my walkabouts in February, I crossed several dozen sets of deer tracks. The route I took proceeded uphill on Harbaugh Road to the west of the game lands fields, then downhill to Drake Run. I crossed the run and worked my way back toward a stand we call the good stand, continuing back across the creek and climbing uphill to camp. On other walkabouts, I would go out through the old clear cut on the south side of Harbaugh Road to the oak flat above the game lands fields. There was never a shortage of deer and turkey tracks on these trips. I also found coyote tracks from time to time, but it seemed that there were not all that many of the "song dogs" in the area. Over the years, we would occasionally hear a pack of them singing. Usually I would not find any bear tracks. With a heavy coating of snow, the bears were sleeping it off in their dens. Winter may be the "mean season" for most wildlife. Bears are spared that inconvenience.

Dave and I were in exploring mode. We took long hikes to learn the lay of the land, hoping to find out where the best hunting in our area of the game lands would be. We did make progress. Some of our exploratory hikes covered four to five miles, and we found a few places that looked promising. During those first years, we ended up hunting farther from the cabin than we needed to. In the future, it would be found that the best hunting is much less than a mile from camp. Dave still had to work for a living, so he could show up only on weekends. Larry and I, being retired, might be in camp anytime.

May brought with it spring gobbler season. Crawford and I hunted turkeys with limited success. Both of us called in birds, but the ones we had shots at were jakes. The mature gobblers made fools out of us. This is the way turkey hunting goes. One interesting incident happened at the lower game commission food plot. (In our early explorations, we had located a large field approximately a half mile from camp. We laughingly refer to this and one other field a short distance away as the "food plots," but the game commission did very little to make them attractive to wildlife.) Crawford had a buddy with him. They were set up at the corner of the field under a huge old white oak tree. As they watched, a sow bear with five cubs crossed the plot, fortunately at a safe distance. The sow and cubs emerged from the woods above the old Harbaugh homestead, located downhill and to the east. We would later place a ladder stand in that hollow.

The feeder Crawford installed attracted a bunch of deer, and the game cameras we put out took many good photos. This proved that we do in fact have some deer around camp. During summer, we had a number of bears frequenting our area. Larry and Avis Guise saw one from the porch of the cabin. A sow with four cubs came in to feed frequently. The amazing thing about this was that both Dave and I hunted bears in northern Pennsylvania for years and had never taken one. Sightings of them in the past were infrequent. Now we were located in what appeared to be prime bear territory. Hopes were high on our part that we could manage to harvest one of these, the most elusive of Pennsylvania big game trophies.

Another project took place that summer. Since the log outer walls of the cabin had never had any sort of treatment, they needed to be stained. We did the higher parts of the walls from a ladder. Sometimes I worked by myself. On one occasion, Nick Sabetto came along and manned a brush. We used the CWF brand of stain recommended by a salesperson in the local Lowes store. (I remain unsatisfied with the results. After a few years, the stain had cracked and peeled. A penetrating oil stain would have been far superior. I hate doing jobs twice when once will suffice.) I must admit that the cabin did look a whole lot better with a coat of stain on it.

Fall brought hunting season, starting with the archery deer season beginning in October. Larry and I hunted most of the month with little success. As was the case when we began to hunt at Camp Bucktail, we were on a learning curve. It takes some time to figure out how to hunt a new territory. Dave Hartman joined us for the early muzzleloader season. During small game season, Casey Ferrell, a teenager who lived next door to my Saint Thomas home, came to camp and took his first pheasant with me.

Casey Ferrell on the left with his first pheasant

Things improved in November with the advent of the rut. Although we saw a few more deer, none of us scored.

During bear season, we had snow on the ground, which was unusual, and made hunting slightly more exciting. Hopes were high that we might harvest a bear, and sign indicated that plenty of them were around. Opening day, the hunters entered the woods and spread out, taking stands in a variety of locations. I picked out a hemlock tree in the saddle along Harbaugh Road, located where we would later put a ladder stand. Early in the morning, I heard the sounds of a drive that was in progress to the west. Perhaps half an hour later, I looked downhill. To my amazement, a sow bear with four cubs was walking uphill on a path which would put her forty yards from my position. I picked up my rifle and took aim, squeezing the trigger, but all that happened was a click. The bolt was not fully engaged. When I squeezed the trigger, the firing pin did not hit the primer hard enough to detonate the cartridge. All five bears took off at a run. The sow was eventually killed by another hunter some distance away. The four cubs stayed in the area and amused us for most of the morning. Crawford did have shooting at another bear, but did not connect.

As an interesting aside, Dave had a group of deer pass his stand, among them a pure albino three-point buck. As he described it, he had trouble making it out in the snow. We would later come to call this buck "Whitey," and he would stimulate a whole lot of interest.

Rifle deer season came in with the usual foul weather, but we did much better this year. Hunting from the good stand, I got a doe the first day. Larry left Craig's lower stand too early, or he might have had a chance at a beautiful buck that our neighbor Scott Hamilton's son shot after it crossed Back Road. On the second day, Dave scored on a doe. Things got more productive for Larry the third day of rifle season. While hunting at the good stand, Larry stuck it out until almost dark. He got two deer; first a doe and then an eight-point buck. This was the first buck taken at Camp Rip-N-Tear. I drove the six-wheeler down to haul his deer out for him. I just had to play a little joke on Larry. When I approached his buck, I called out to him, "Nice four-point, Larry." A four point would not be a legal buck since antler restrictions went into effect. Larry was really disappointed until I told him, "That is a four-point, western count." Out west they count only one side of a deer's rack, so a buck with four points on each side is called a four-point. Nick awakened from a nap and took a doe while hunting with us the second Tuesday. I guess five deer in one rifle season wasn't too bad for us since we were still learning how to hunt our area.

Larry with his double

Nick, Dave, and Larry with the "after the nap" doe

2009: The "Whitey" Year

The hunting year began, as usual, with wintertime scouting. I went to camp frequently during the winter to download photos from the trail cameras we have out. Some pretty nice bucks and a whole lot of turkeys were in the pictures. All of the bucks eventually lose their antlers, but some hold on to them longer than others. We have seen bucks that have lost them during rifle deer season and some that are still holding them in March or April. I wonder what makes the difference. It looked as though spring gobbler season would be a great one, and hopes were high for the fall hunting seasons as well. One of the bucks seen in our photos and occasionally coming in to the feeder next to the cabin was a pure albino. Dave had been the first to see him the previous fall during bear season. After that, several of us saw him during the bear and deer seasons, but he was only a three-point and not legal. There was snow on the ground after mid-November, so seeing him was really tough. We decided to name him Whitey.

In this photo, Whitey has already lost one antler. His buddy still has both of his.

The second trout opener came upon us, and I had resolved to relearn fly fishing this year. In early spring, I purchased a fly rod with all the bells and whistles. There are several stocked trout streams in the area of the cabin, and the stream running past camp, Glade Run, has a good population of native brook trout. During the first week of trout season, I fished both the Laurel Hill Creek and the Youghiogheny, catching a few from time to time. I did try to teach a few worms to swim in Glade and Alex Runs. While the native brook trout are small, they always seem to be hungry. We learn more about camp every year, it seems. Who would have known it would be a fisherman's dream?

During the spring gobbler season, both Crawford and I called in birds, but again, most were jakes. The mature gobblers that showed up either hung up beyond shotgun range or made fools of us. No birds were taken, but a lot of fun was had. I sometimes wonder if a bird with a brain the size of a walnut isn't one of the smartest animals on the planet. We did most of our turkey hunting between the cabin and the game lands fields. One place about halfway to the fields was a crossing frequently used by turkeys and deer. A huge blowdown marks this spot. It makes a decent place to park one's posterior and see what transpires. We later put a ladder stand close to this. Of course, we named it the blowdown stand.

A summer project involved closing in the back porch and converting it into a bunkroom complete with two sets of bunk beds. Crawford did most of the exterior carpentry work. I did some of the finish carpentry and painting inside. It makes for a cold bunkroom during winter, but some of us prefer that to hot. We purchased cheap mattresses for the bunk beds from a Big Lots store in Chambersburg. These proved to be pretty poor quality, so we immediately considered looking for replacements. Hopefully, the offer of free mattresses would again come from Saint Francis University in Loretto, Pennsylvania. It seemed to happen annually on the message board huntingpa.com.

Another major camp improvement project began this year. This actually started the previous year. One day that summer while I was in camp, Richard Sabo showed up with a guy who was hired to survey his two-acre plot next to our land. I introduced myself to him. He turned out to be Jeff Ripple, the engineer who had done the plot map for our property. I talked with him awhile and later decided to get in contact again. We eventually hired his firm, J. Ripple & Associates, to engineer a sewage system for us. Mr. Ripple engaged a soils scientist, Ron Andrasko, to pick a site for a sand mound. One was found on the hillside toward Back Road. Mr. Ripple marked the area and gave us instructions as to how much we had to clear. Dave, Larry, Nick, and I set about cutting down all the trees on the proposed site. I took my tractor out to camp and dragged logs, piling them next to the shed so that we could cut them up later. There would be plenty of firewood for the next few years.

When Mr. Ripple's firm completed the work, he submitted plans to our sewage enforcement officer, Reggie Musser. Mr. Musser showed up one day to do percolation testing, which the site passed, and we finally got the go-ahead to begin construction. We requested bids from several firms. When the bids came in, we contracted with Svonavek Excavating to do the work on our new system. From start to finish, nearly two years passed until this whole process was completed.

I took a break from hunting at the cabin during the third week of October and went to visit Hugh Walters' outfit in South Carolina. He calls it Deerfield Plantation, a name it gets honestly. Plenty of deer are found there. I went with two guys I met on the huntingpa.com message board. John Moliterni hails from New Jersey, and this would be the second hunt I shared with him. Steve Musser from the Harrisburg area has hunted with Hugh for many years and finally talked me into going on this one. Steve got the nicest buck of the week, tagging a huge old eight-point. I managed to take two bucks, one a decent eight-point. John actually shot two bucks on one stand! The first one turned out to be a pretty nice eight-point. The other was somewhat smaller. Well, back to Pennsylvania.

While I was away in South Carolina, Svonavec Excavating installed our new sand mound system and hooked up the cabin drain lines for us. They were putting the finishing touches on it when I returned. When the work was finished, sewage enforcement officer Reggie Musser did his final inspection and told me, "You now have a legal cabin." The water system had yet to be hooked up to provide running water, but progress toward a livable camp certainly was being made.

The only hunter to hunt at camp during the early muzzleloader doe season was Dave, and he got the job done. On Friday of that week, he scored on a nice doe while hunting out of what Rick Steinmiller called the metal stand. Rick had two more or less permanent stands. One is constructed out of wood a short distance downhill from his cabin. The other is the metal stand, located near the game lands boundary on Rick Sabo's tract. Larry took a week off and went on an elk hunt in Montana. He came home with lots of camp meat from a nice bull elk.

During the last few weeks of archery season, I decided to limit my hunting to the albino buck. He kept appearing in the same spots, so it was just a matter of time until I crossed paths with him, or so I thought. The first day of fall turkey season, Crawford came to camp. We decided to go turkey hunting. Lousy choice on my part. While carrying the shotgun, I caught a glimpse of something white coming through the woods on my right. Sure enough, the albino crossed the logging road twenty yards in front of me. When I grunted, he stopped broadside to me and pawed the ground. It would have been a "can't miss" shot with my crossbow. So it goes when we commit hunting. If we were always successful, it would probably be called shopping, wouldn't it?

I did not see the albino again until the last Friday of archery season. I was hunting the good stand in the hollow below camp. He crossed behind and about thirty yards from me. I managed to take a shot, but split a sapling instead of burying the broadhead behind the shoulder where it was definitely headed. There are times that if I didn't have bad luck, I wouldn't have any luck at all. That was my one chance at the albino. I was not too terribly displeased. At least I had a chance. (I hope the guy who got him the second day of rifle season realizes just how lucky he is.)

Later on, the first archery bear season ever held found Larry and me in camp. Larry had a new spot he wanted to try, so I went back to the good stand from which I had the chance at Whitey. About fifteen minutes after it got light enough to see, I noticed movement in the laurel thicket to the east and concentrated on that. It turned out to be a huge old boar bear, probably in the 500-pound range. I got so excited that I made a major mistake and used the wrong sight pin. The arrow went under his ribs and buried itself in the forest floor. At the shot, the bruin jumped up and turned toward me. With the crossbow, there is no chance at a second shot. He slowly ambled off into the woods. Of course, I had a bad case of the shakes. I have killed five black bears, all in Canada, but this one really got to me, adrenalin wise. I don't think I have been so excited on wild game ever before, and I have hunted a whole lot in my lifetime. When I stop getting excited about seeing a trophy animal, I think I will quit hunting.

Sunday, November 22, found a bunch of us in camp. Crawford, Larry, Dave, Dave's nephew Judd, Mike McCullough (my favorite taxidermist), and Crawford's brother-in-law Stan were here to pursue bruins. I cooked up a huge roasting pan full of sauerkraut, kielbasa, and pork, along with plenty of mashed potatoes. After due consideration, perhaps it wasn't such a great idea after all because the stuff caused major intestinal distress. That was putting it mildly. My recipe is now world renowned, due to the seismic effect of the explosions, particularly Dave's.

We hunted the first two days of bear season without spotting a bear, but we did see a bunch of deer. Judd got some cell phone photos of Whitey and several other bucks. Mike, Stan, and Crawford each saw a huge nine-point buck chasing a doe. I encountered a large buck that was nearly totally grey in color. I thought he was an eight-point because he had two points up off the main beam, but the rack appeared smaller than it should be for a deer that size. Although we did not accomplish our goal of taking the first Camp Rip-N-Tear bear, we saw plenty of game to keep us interested, including one big bobcat sighted by Dave while he hunted at Craig's wooden stand. As he watched, it caught a chipmunk.

Rifle deer season is always a great time for us. Dave and I got to camp late on Saturday, and Larry joined us on Sunday. I worked up a twenty-quart pot of venison stew for us to chew on the next couple of days, and we spent Sunday checking zeros on our rifles, watching football on TV, and swapping lies. This is what deer camp is all about, isn't it? The weather forecast was not the best. Heavy rain and windy conditions were on the menu for the first morning. Dave decided to hunt the stand he placed about three quarters of a mile from camp. Larry had a stand set up in the hollow to the south of camp. I hunted the good stand from which I had the shot at Whitey and the bear. I hoped to be comfortable enough because I put up a tree umbrella to shield me from the worst of the rain, but the wind kept raising the tree umbrella and dumping water down the back of my neck. I have seldom hunted on a more miserable day in my fifty-six years of pursuing whitetails in Pennsylvania.

About 8:00 AM, I spied a large deer coming through the brush from the north of my stand. I saw antlers and counted two points up off the main beams. This appeared to be the gray deer I had seen in bear season. While the rack was not the biggest, I decided that enough of this rain had gone down my back, so I raised the rifle and took the shot he presented when he crossed the creek thirty yards from me. He ran about twenty yards and piled up.

When I got to the deer, I have to admit I was a bit disappointed, because instead of an eight-point, I had taken a six. His antlers had no brow tines. The antlers were thick in diameter but short in length. His coat was as gray as a mule deer buck's coat would be. I tagged and field dressed him before grabbing an antler to begin the drag to camp. That is when I realized he was a really big deer. After struggling for twenty minutes dragging him to our property line just fifty or so yards away, I decided to walk back to camp and get the six-wheeler to haul him out. I used the game commission's chest tape to estimate his weight at 171 pounds dressed (with the entrails removed) and nearly 210 pounds live weight. This is more deer than I expected, given the small rack. Several years later, my friend Kathy Davis (who is an expert in such things) looked at a jaw I had removed from this buck and determined by tooth wear that he was either four or five years old. It is strange a buck that age would have such a small rack. Perhaps we could chalk this up to genetic potential. Concerning antler growth, this buck did not have it.

Since we all had doe tags, we were not done. My buck was the only one killed during the two-week season. We hunted hard but unproductively for the rest of the first week. On Tuesday of the second week, we had a really good day. Three decent sized does came in to the meat pole, so we spent the next day butchering and grinding meat. We concluded that would be enough for this season. Besides, the weather comedian had forecast a big storm moving in on Thursday, so we decided to beat it home.

The post-Christmas primitive weapons season was really special for me. I hunted at Camp Bucktail with my buddies John Bartholow and Larry Dubbs. We were joined by Bill Lloyd who had just returned from a tour of duty in Iraq with his Pennsylvania National Guard unit. Bill brought his sons Will and Mike along. We worked like heck to see if we could get Bill a deer. He had opportunities, but it just didn't happen. The funny thing was that we saw plenty of deer and a lot of sign in an area where guys are griping about there not being any of either. Next year would be another year, and in the words of the Bard, "Hope springs eternal in the human breast," so we planned to be out there doing it again.

TWO YEARS WITH WHITEY

This story is about our encounter with a special whitetail buck, one of the most rare and beautiful woodland creatures that Mother Nature in her infinite wisdom sometimes creates. We named him Whitey. He was a pure albino whitetail buck, the only one I have ever seen in my fifty-seven years of hunting and pursuing nature's wonders. We have the Pennsylvania Game Commission to thank for the fact that we got to enjoy him for two years. Since 2002, antler restrictions have allowed us to take only bucks with three points to one antler, and as a yearling, Whitey did not qualify.

We first knew of Whitey's existence during bear season of 2008. In addition to seeing our first bears since buying the camp, and actually having shooting at them, Dave Hartman reported that he had seen a totally white deer, a three-point buck. We have learned not to question Dave's eagle eyes. What he sees is nearly always accurately described. I did talk to another hunter who had seen Whitey, and apparently from my conversations with him, the local residents knew of his existence.

During the following winter, we had a trail camera out at one of the two feeders we stock with corn. On three consecutive days, the camera took photos of this wonderful deer. On the first day, February second, he had both antlers, one a small Y and the other a spike, thus confirming Dave's observation that snowy November day. On February third, he had lost the spike, and February fourth, he shed the Y, thus leaving him bald for the balance of winter. Later in March, we got two photos of him, usually with his buddy who was a normally colored buck that had been a four-point the past fall.

Summer came, and the bucks started to grow antlers. We saw Whitey several times during summer, but he managed not to have his photo snapped by our trail cameras. By this time, we had four trail cameras in place. Usually I would get a glimpse of him while scouting, and occasionally I would see him crossing the road near our camp, but I never had a camera ready when that happened. By August, it was obvious that he would be either a seven-point or an eight-point. Several of the local folks saw him, so I started to worry that our local poachers would get him before an ethical hunter could take him legally during hunting season. I wanted that hunter to be me. I made a vow to myself that if I were that lucky hunter, I would spring for a full body mount from my taxidermist, Mike McCullough.

I restricted my hunting during October's archery deer season. I hunted only for Whitey, passing up several chances at other bucks. One day, a neighbor, Jim Procyson stopped by while riding his mountain bike. Our conversation quickly turned to the subject of our albino buck. Jim told me his wife was adamant about not wanting anyone to kill him. She had almost taken ownership. I told Jim that unfortunately I could not cooperate, and if the opportunity presented itself, I would certainly try to harvest him.

My first real opportunity at him was one I blew big time. By the first Friday of November, the bucks were in what I call the searching/walking phase where they are covering territory in search of hot does. Crawford came to camp to hunt turkeys, so I gave the archery hunting a break and took the shotgun for a walk. You guessed it. While walking along a forest road, I caught a glimpse of white traveling parallel to the road. I kneeled down in the middle of the road just as he crossed in front of me, and I made a noise that sounds to me like a sheep bleating. He stopped, stared directly at me, and pawed the ground less than twenty yards ahead of me. My shotgun was the wrong weapon for this encounter. Had I been carrying my crossbow, the shot would have been easy, but this was not to be.

The next and last opportunity I had to harvest Whitey came on the final Friday of archery season. I was set up in the good stand. This sixteen foot ladder stand is located along a creek bottom less than a quarter mile from our cabin. A frequently used crossing is thirty yards from its base, and I have taken two bucks from this stand the past two years. At 8:00 that morning, I saw a flash of white along the hillside above the stand. Whitey was on a collision course that would take him behind my stand, so I turned to be in position for a shot if one presented itself. It did! At a distance of less than thirty yards, he stopped broadside to me when I grunted. I put the thirty-yard dot on the sweet spot behind the shoulder and squeezed the trigger of my Ten Point Titan crossbow, sending a bolt on its way. It was heading true when its path intersected with a sapling I had not seen, so hard was I concentrating on the aim and shot. The Wasp Jackhammer broadhead nearly felled the one inch sapling, and Whitey exited the area at a trot. I was left with a huge feeling of disappointment, knowing that might be the last chance for me to harvest him. This premonition proved to be true.

Two weeks later, the first day of rifle season began with a pouring rain and brisk winds. After two hours of rain going down my back, I decided that the first legal buck to walk past my stand would be mine. Shortly after I reached that decision, a big six-point made a fatal mistake. My buck hunting was over for that season. I found out later that another hunter had killed Whitey when a neighbor, Hank Steinmiller, told me he saw two hunters dragging a white deer out of the woods.

One day the following August, Jim Procyson stopped by camp to visit. He told me he had seen the buck hanging and knew the hunter who harvested him. I prevailed upon Jim to let that hunter know I would like to meet him and would greatly appreciate any photos he might have. I eventually got caught up in the fervor of archery deer season and forgot about my request. On Tuesday, November 9, I harvested a nice eight-point buck with my crossbow and then commenced to get excited about the five-day archery bear season and subsequent rifle bear season. All thoughts of Whitey passed into the long-term storage section of my memory.

December came, and with it, rifle deer season. While we were in camp one day, a guy named Vince Paola showed up to visit. Vince hunts from a camp half a mile north of us along Back Road. He identified himself as the hunter who harvested the albino eight-point. It seems Whitey had three measurable points on his right antler and five on his left. He promised to email me the photos he has of this beautiful buck and the mount his taxidermist did of it. True to his word, I received an email from Vince on

Sunday, December 5, with a whole bunch of photos showing Whitey on his final day and the mount his taxidermist, Pat Ashbaugh of Nowrytown, had done for him. This gave me closure for one of the greatest stories of my hunting career. After all, even though I was not as lucky as Vince had been, I felt blessed to have enjoyed my two years with Whitey and hope the reader can get some vicarious enjoyment of this beautiful creature as well. You don't have to be the successful hunter to have enjoyed the hunt, do you?

Vince Paola's mount of Whitey

2010: *Camp Rip-N-Tear Goes Modern*

Sometime in January, things started to go downhill in a big way, weather wise. We had one of the worst winters in recent memory with lots of snow. While there was a tolerable amount of snow at my home in Saint Thomas, the Laurel Highlands really got hit, and hit hard. According to our neighbor Bill Ream, one big January snowstorm dropped over three feet of snow. Dave and I went to the cabin on January 21 prepared to plow the driveway only to find that the snow had compacted during a brief warm spell following the storm. The driveway was relatively open. We drove right up to camp without plowing at all. We experimented a bit with snowshoes borrowed from Nick Sabetto and found that they worked pretty well in a foot of wet snow. There were lots of deer tracks and even one set of bear tracks on Harbaugh Road in the state game lands, leading us to believe that plenty of deer survived hunting season. We were already getting pumped up for next fall.

Things went further downhill in February. Two huge snows hit our Somerset camp, and at one point we had close to five feet of snow on the ground. When I called from home to check on the situation, Mrs. Ream asked me if we had been to our cabin and shoveled our roof. I told her we had not. She replied, "Oh, my." This got me to worrying about the structural integrity of the roof, so Dave and I hitched up the trailer, loaded the tractor, and drove out to camp on March 3. What we found was that while the snow had compacted somewhat, it was still over three feet deep in the driveway. I began to plow with the tractor. Dave put on snowshoes and hiked up the hill to camp. I got the tractor stuck three times while plowing the driveway. Dave shoveled the snow off the porch and opened a path from the shed to the cabin.

The weight of the snow nearly collapsed the roof over the back porch. We put some temporary bracing in place to keep it from caving in. At least we intended it to be temporary. (The roof over the porch would not be permanently fixed until seven years had gone by. We finally got around to it during summer of 2017.)

Dave stands in the path he shoveled from the shed to the cabin

What simply amazed us was that a bunch of animals were making it to our feeder. One photo showed a group of six bucks visiting it at one time. The turkeys seemed to have less trouble navigating on top of the snow. Maybe they had evolved snowshoes? It was almost funny to watch them take several steps on top of the snow, hit a soft spot and sink nearly out of sight, then struggle back to the surface. The deer, being longer in the leg category, had paths where they had broken through the snow to get there. Because the deer would be at low ebb in their fat reserves, we decided to skip walkabouts to find out where they were hiding. We did not want to make them use any more energy than absolutely necessary.

Spring finally arrived! The snow melted, and we could get around to do inventory of game populations, download the photos from our trail cameras, and fill the feeders. We discovered another problem. Ice damming caused water to back up under the shingles and leak through the roof. We would have to correct this. (We tried several things, but would eventually decide the only way to fix it would be a new roof, as previously mentioned.)

The turkey population seemed to be great with a whole lot of turkeys surviving the winter in good shape. By April, gobblers were sounding off in the morning. Crawford and I hit the woods for the May opener of spring gobbler season and met with mixed success. We both succeeded in calling gobblers in, but did not score. One huge gobbler hung up for Crawford just out of shotgun range, and I had one of the strong, silent type come in without warning gobbles.

Trout fishing was a bit more successful. I managed to catch some the first day and several other times. Fly fishing the Yough resulted in a few nice trout being caught and released. I also fished in Glade Run which borders Craig Sabo's property. A good population of native brookies that live there are always hungry.

Winter grudgingly gives way to spring at camp.

Memorial Day weekend saw Doris and me joining the Peters family in camp. Crawford and I did some camp chores. Doris and I went for a hike along Little Glade and Alex Runs to the south of camp. I snapped the following photo of Doris at a waterfall along Alex Run.

Doris at a Glade Run waterfall

Doris and Crawford's dog Monk find the porch of the cabin to be a great place to relax.

Up until this point, we had not hooked up the pressure water system. Crawford and I did this part of the plumbing one weekend in June. We installed a hot water heater, a double filter system, and water lines to the kitchen and bathroom sinks. Now we could take hot showers. We also hooked up the Sir Thomas Crapper (He was knighted by the queen for his invention of the flush toilet. You can look it up.) water closet, which would make the morning constitutional a more comfortable thing. The place was now in good enough shape that it could be someone's home. We still needed to avoid having pipes freeze during the later hunting seasons.

During late July, Crawford and Karen hosted their biker gang for a camp outing. Two huge thunderstorms earlier in the month wreaked havoc with the driveway, and I had to bring my tractor out to do major re-grading the weekend of July 24-25. Crawford, Karen, and the two kids showed up Friday evening with an air conditioner on the hitch carrier of their Cherokee. It turned out that this was the air conditioner found on the back porch of the cabin when we bought it. Crawford took it home to check it out, and it worked. Sleeping was a lot more comfortable those two nights. On Saturday, Crawford and I began erecting his Cadillac stand in the hollow. We set four corner posts in concrete. The stand would be built on these about ten feet from the property line with SGL 111. After the posts were set, I used the tractor to collect some of the firewood Dave and I had cut back in the fall and pile it for splitting. The plan was to do this sometime in November when we have a gang at camp.

On Sunday, I took the tractor down to the road that goes past the food plot along the stream with the idea of using it and the chainsaw to open the road so we have access to that area. It took about two hours of pushing out laurel bushes, but the road is now open. We cut down a bunch of trees and pushed out shrubs to make a food plot across the creek from the first ladder stand.   I finished the job of clearing and planting the food plot area across the creek the following weekend (July 31-August 1). We could now get into that area with the six-wheeler. Let's see if it grows. (Maybe we will get some rain?)

Early in August, I made a trip to Saint Francis College in Loretto, PA. Dean Dietrich, the physical plant manager of the college, again made an offer on the huntingpa.com website for free twin sized mattresses to any hunting camp that wanted them. I picked up eight really decent and only slightly used ones. They are great. Thanks, Dean. We junked those el cheapo mattresses. Dean also gave us a couple of double decker bunk beds which we separated to make single beds of twin size. With six single and two full size beds upstairs, and two double decker bunk beds on the back porch, we were now set up for a gang during hunting season.

Larry and I went to camp on Friday, August 13. We swapped lies, downloaded some photos from the trail cameras, and watched a football game. One of the bucks that visited the feeder near the cabin looked really promising! The following photo was taken shortly before he shed his velvet, two weeks later.

A really promising eight-point in velvet

On Saturday, Larry tried to locate the perfect place for a ladder stand that he found during the 2009 deer season. First, he hiked to his stand at the hemlock tree past the PGC food plots and checked things out there. Then he walked around in circles looking for that previously mentioned perfect spot, but did not find it. Meanwhile, I decided to work on the woodpile. I cut up some of the big logs we hauled and stacked behind the shed. When Larry got back, we worked them up with the wood splitter. On Sunday morning, I walked out to the game lands with Larry, and we did manage to find that perfect place. Once we did, we tied some orange markers on a path leading to it so he could find it again. Larry took off for home later on Sunday morning, leaving me to my own devices for the rest of the day. Maybe he should have stayed around one more evening. At 6:00 PM, the bear in the following photo came in and nearly walked up to the porch. I was wondering if I should be getting nervous.

Crawford and his family went to camp over the Labor Day weekend, and he put a few more hours into the construction of his Cadillac stand (which we later renamed the condo) in the hollow below camp. He prefabricated the rest of it at home and then brought it out to camp later to finish it.

The archery opener, October 2, found Larry and me in camp. Hopes were high for a great season, due to the nice photos we were getting from the game cameras. Some deer were seen, but not what we wanted to harvest just yet. A highlight was that Chad Steinmiller took a shot at a young buck while hunting from the good stand that first evening. He missed. Larry and I found his arrow the next day. Rain came Monday through Wednesday of the next week, thus limiting the amount of time these two old codgers wanted to spend in the woods.

Once again, I had a trip to South Carolina planned for the third week of October, so my time in camp was cut short that month. However, the week was a huge success, and I brought home enough venison and pork for this year. One of the bucks I got is among the best I have ever taken.

Really nice South Carolina eight-point with guide Kevin Reeves on the left

The last week of October was somewhat disappointing. The rut really hadn't kicked in yet. Very few scrapes and rubs were being found, and this led us to believe the rut would be later than usual. Cold weather arrived that week. Temperatures dropped to the twenties and thirties overnight with highs in the forties and fifties during the day. The weather forecast indicated snow showers toward the end of the week.

November heralded the beginning of the rut. Some of the bucks were now out walking and searching for does. I did see the big eight-point again while hunting near the blowdown stand. Larry also saw him while hunting from a stand close to Back Road on Craig's property. Tuesday of the second week in November brought the first kill for camp this year. I managed to luck into an eight-point that made a fatal mistake, standing broadside along the creek at the good stand long enough for me to shoot. As seems to be the usual case, he came from the area of a short tributary of Drake Run. This stream has its origin along Back Road close to Jersey Hollow Road. Deer feeding in Waley's fields enter the woods downhill from the Steinmiller camp, then make their way across Back Road on to Richard Sabo's tract and downhill toward that tributary. They follow it to where it joins Drake Run in the vicinity of the stand.

Another path, an old logging road that parallels Drake Run and passes the good stand at a distance of forty yards, is a second preferred route for game animals. It was on this that I had shooting at the huge bear a year ago. I have also seen foxes, a coyote, and even one fisher while in that stand. Some of the animals using this route come from the Ream fields which are a short distance to the south of Waley's farm.

Bear season came in with five days of archery bear hunting this year followed by the opening of rifle bear season on Saturday. Larry and I hunted the first day, but rain sent us home to work on our honeydo lists until Thursday. Dave showed up on Friday to hunt with his new crossbow, and Crawford also arrived. We hunted the three days of rifle season. Not a single bear was sighted, but the big boar who hung around camp left us his calling card on Sunday night in the form of a large pile of bear scat fifty feet from the cabin porch. We had no idea where he slept during the daytime. On Monday, we drove the laurel patches on each side of the camp and also pushed out the swamp. The only game sighted were two deer, one of which was a big buck that a driver almost stepped on. We discussed placing a ladder stand in the laurel on Craig's property, as the sign was plentiful there.

Rifle deer season found Larry and Dave hunting with me serving as camp cook since our area was bucks only for the first five days. As is usually the case, I worked up a huge pot of stew and also cooked a few other meals as the guys requested them. On the first day of rifle season, our neighbor Scott Hamilton arrived at the place he wanted to be a bit later than anticipated. Without intending to, he pushed a nice five-point out toward Dave who made a heck of a shot on it. Two young hunters at the Steinmiller camp were also successful. Ricky Sabo took his first buck, a nice five-point, and Hank Steinmiller bagged a huge eight-point that weighed 174 pounds dressed. Dave and I helped Hank retrieve his deer. We dragged it to our property line and then loaded it on the six-wheeler. That made the rest of the trip to the Steinmiller camp a whole lot easier.

No other deer were taken that first week. Dave and I went to the DMAP area on Mount Davis a couple of days. The weather was typical for Mount Davis with a blizzard in progress and wind chill factors near zero. We were able to locate a concentration of deer in one location. The only possible shot was when I kicked out a doe on the way back to the truck (having had enough of nearly freezing to death). I opted not to take the shot as it would have been across a road, which could have been a dangerous shot.

Ricky Sabo and Hank Steinmiller pose with their first day bucks.

Dave and I hunted a few days during the second week at Camp Bucktail. Larry had to take the second week off from hunting to assist his wife Avis after knee surgery. The only kill that week was made by neighbor Terry Dennis on the last day. Never give up. We also found out that Bill Lloyd finally got his first buck on the opening day of rifle season at Camp Bucktail. Congratulations, Bill.

2011: *Our First Spring Gobblers*

After a successful deer season during which we took two bucks for the first time, and the usual bear season in which we saw none, 2011 began with great promise. (For some strange reason, every year seems to begin with a lot of promise, but I digress.) There existed several good reasons for such confidence. The trail cameras at our feeders yielded some photos of bucks that survived the fall season, including a great looking nine-point. He held on to his antlers until sometime in March. Winter inventory disclosed a lot of sign. The tracks in the snow gave testimony to decent populations of deer and turkeys. Such things do not lie. The game was there.

I made the trip out to the cabin a number of times during the winter to check on things and look for sign of game. Dave was working full-time as a mason and Larry had some issues he needed to work through, so most of those times I was by myself. The feeder next to the cabin attracted a bunch of turkeys, and a dozen or so deer were regular visitors during the rough part of winter. They continued doing this well into spring. Some of the turkeys that came in to the feeder were nice longbeards. This gave us high hopes for spring gobbler season. Late in April, a sow bear with four cubs showed up to feed, and a huge old boar left his calling card. We got no really good photos of them, but deer and turkeys kept showing up. During much of the winter, I stocked the feeder with a combination of corn and oats. The turkeys seemed to prefer the oats to the corn, while the deer concentrated on the corn.

The first week of spring gobbler season, Doris and I took a long weekend vacation at Williamsburg. Crawford and his brother-in-law Stan were the only hunters in camp. What a time they had! As Crawford told it, when they arrived at camp, Stan found a huge pile of bear scat next to the front porch. He picked it up with a shovel to pitch it down the hill behind the cabin and found a lot more there. He called Crawford to see the piles of scat. While they were there, a sow and her four yearling cubs walked right up the ATV path from the bottom of the hollow. They lost sight of the family of bears, so the two of them continued to unload the truck and take their things into the cabin. The sow and her cubs came past them on Craig Sabo's side of the drive as they finished unloading. Seeing this family of bears gave them a real thrill. Just thirty years ago, there were no bears at all in Somerset County.

By the time they got up the next morning, it was already light enough to see. After a hurried breakfast of sorts, Stan went down into the hollow near the condo while Crawford walked a short distance up the road toward the PGC food plots. He didn't get too far when the gobbling erupted. He heard a whole bunch of gobblers sounding off. Shortly after that, he heard one shot from Stan's direction. A few seconds later a gobbler ran past him, but it happened too quickly for him to get off a shot. He moved up the road to his favorite place by the blowdown and set up to call. With the first few yelps, a gobbler answered. Within a few minutes, a pair of red heads showed up. He shot the first one to give him a clean shot. Crawford's turkey season was over.

Stan, with the results of a good morning

When Crawford returned to camp, he called Stan on the radio. Stan replied, "I've got a problem." It turned out that when Stan shot at the first gobbler to raise his head above a log, he actually got two of them with one shot. Both birds being mature gobblers, he had quite a load to carry uphill to the cabin. Crawford snapped the above photo of the happy hunter and his trophies. Stan took the biggest one to Mac's taxidermy shop to be mounted. This was Stan's first spring gobbler kill, and these turkeys were the first spring kills for Camp Rip-N-Tear. Congratulations to both guys were in order. I think it happened this way, but don't ask me to testify in court. I was not there at the time.

The weekend of May 6-9, Dave and I went to camp, hoping to hunt gobblers on Saturday morning. As is our custom, we sat on the porch to listen for gobbles and decide where we should hunt, but not a peep was heard. It is legal to hunt gobblers during the spring season only until noon. After hunting for a short time, we quit mid-morning and spent the rest of the day planting some seedlings and doing a few camp chores. Rick Steinmiller came to camp that evening, and we had a great dinner of fried chicken. Dave left for home Sunday morning. I stayed over Sunday night and was awakened at 4:00 AM by a crash on the front porch. Our resident bear decided to turn over the gas grille. By the time I got to the front door, he was gone. While the grille survived without major damage, he made quite a mess on our porch, giving me one additional chore for the next morning.

The rainy season of April and May brought a lot more rain than usual. As a result, not many hen turkeys raised broods of chicks. This would probably impact our hunting for the fall season, and maybe even next spring. Hen turkeys who nest are at the mercy of whatever weather occurs. There are other hazards. Bears will raid a nest and eat the eggs. Bobcats and coyotes are major predators. It is amazing that turkeys are as numerous as they usually are, given what they must overcome to produce a hatch of poults.

On one of my visits to camp during the month of July, I noticed that the excavation for our sewer system done the previous year damaged the roots of a red oak tree next to the cabin. This tree had two trunks of eighteen inches or so in diameter, and one leaned over the cabin. Both needed to be taken down. I wasn't sure whether we could do the job or if we should hire a tree removal service to do it. Severe thunderstorms hit the area on Thursday, July 28. The driveway washed out again. A maple tree in Scott Hamilton's front yard split and fell, hanging up on another tree. It was indeed lucky that it didn't land on his cabin.

Rick Steinmiller reported that several nice bucks were coming out into the soybean field next to his cabin to feed in the evening. He named one Frank the Tank because he was so huge. Rick said he was a typical ten-point; probably the big eight-point nobody got last year. As I remembered it, this buck came past my stand during bear season the previous year. At the time, I was mightily impressed with his antlers. As I watched, he ran out of the laurel close to the rock stand and stopped to check his back trail less than thirty yards from the rock ledge on which I was sitting. I wondered at the time what he would look like in another year, and we found that out.

During spring, I planted a bunch of seedlings. Two of them were American chestnut that I got from the Pennsylvania chapter of the American Chestnut Foundation. They are supposed to be blight tolerant. I guess we will know in ten years or so whether or not they are. I also planted a bunch of apple, crabapple, and shagbark hickory seedlings. Time will tell how they turn out. At the time, things looked pretty good. (We would later find that the chestnut seedlings all died, making this experiment a failure. At least we tried, right?)

The second weekend in August found Larry and me in camp. We put up the rock and blowdown stands, took a long walk to check salt licks, and ended up at the third food plot. Sign looked good for deer season. We downloaded the photos from the game cameras. Evidently there were a large number of deer and a few bears coming in to our food plots near the cabin.

A very unusual ten-point that we never saw again

During the latter part of August, a really strange looking buck showed up. His coat was very grey in color. He had the weirdest antler configuration I have ever seen. He was actually a ten-point, but one of the most unusual ten points you will ever see. Each side of his antlers had three brow tines. It seems that we may have two color phases of deer in our hunting area, grey and brown.

September slowly came to an end. Although his birthday is actually October 4, Crawford's 50th birthday party was scheduled for the Saturday before archery deer season (a week early) for obvious reasons. Normally it would not actually take place until archery season had begun, but we couldn't interfere with something that important. A great time was had by all at the McConnellsburg American Legion picnic grounds, his birthday well-celebrated.

Larry and I spent the entire first week of archery deer season in camp. While we did see some deer, the rain continued for the first four days, so we didn't hunt much at all. Rick Steinmiller, our neighbor, killed a nice doe the first morning at ten o'clock. He said he was just about wet enough to quit when a group of eight does and fawns came past the metal stand. For some strange reason, I again saw more deer than Larry. I suspect he misses some that go past him, especially when they come from directions he is not expecting. Larry went home on Sunday. I stayed over the weekend and hunted Monday morning of the second week before going home. For the seven days, I saw a total of thirty deer, four of which were bucks. No shots presented themselves to either of us. Larry did see two bears, while Rick and I each saw one. Chad Steinmiller, Rick's youngest son, got his first archery kill on the second Saturday, a nice doe.

On Sunday, I got invited to a cookout at Scott Hamilton's camp. Being of Scottish descent, Scott and his friends had formed a bagpipe band. It was there to prepare for and march in the local pumpkin festival parade. The pumpkin festival is the high point of the year in Confluence. Later in the day I went into Confluence to visit the festival and watch the parade.

I took a week off and traveled to South Carolina's Deerfield Plantation again this year. While the weather was hot the first three days and the hunting was slow, it cooled off for the end of the hunt. I managed to take two bucks and a doe. One of the bucks was really nice, an eight-point with a fourteen-inch spread that weighed 170 pounds.

I returned to camp late in the afternoon on Wednesday, October 26. Dave joined me Friday afternoon. Crawford and Stan arrived later in the evening. Snow began just before dark. By morning, we had about five inches of the wet and sloppy kind. Hunting was, to say the least, an adventure. Gobs of snow cascaded down from the treetops and made hunting difficult, but several of us saw deer. By 10:30, all were out of the woods except for Dave who stayed out longer. This was more proof that winter weather could come anytime in Somerset County.

After lunch, we decided to take down the two dead trees that were hanging over the cabin. Stan climbed a ladder and attached a rope to the first trunk. We added some chains and a come-along to guide it, tied the rope to the tractor to pull, and dropped it exactly where we wanted. The same process was repeated on the second trunk with similar results. We planned a wood splitting work day for the Sunday of bear season, weather permitting. After the guys left for home on Sunday, I cut the trunks into six long logs and used the tractor to haul and stack them. I also cut up some of the tops and stacked more wood on the porch.

The rut kicked in the last week of October. On Thursday morning of that week, a group of three does made a wrong decision just as it became light enough to shoot and fed past the good stand. When the largest one gave me an opportunity, I made a clean kill.

Saturday, November 5, I took my rifle out for a walk, hoping to harvest a turkey. Upon entering the woods above the second PGC food plot, a herd of ten does and one really decent eight-point broke cover and ran across the oak flat where I hunted the first year we had the cabin. I decided to set up a stand there, so on Sunday I packed an old brown ladder stand in. Of course, the name we gave to this stand is the brown stand. I sat on it one time the last day of archery deer season, but the wind was all wrong. I saw only one squirrel, so I moved it to what I thought would be a better location for rifle bear season.

Tuesday of the last week of archery season, Larry got lucky and harvested a doe. We butchered it and froze the meat in the back porch refrigerator. I dropped off his meat at Grove's butcher shop the following Monday, November 14. The rut then seemed to pause, and we saw very few deer. I did see two bears during that week, but there seemed to be no sign of bears after that. Hopefully this would change during bear season, but things didn't look promising. The last week of archery deer season turned out to be a real disappointment. While Larry did manage toharvest another doe, buck sightings were slim. It was warm, and the rut obviously had not kicked in as evidenced by the lack of the usual rubs and scrapes. We moved Larry's ladder stand to a tree close to the big rock. For awhile, we called this rock "Steve's rock," since Mr. Sabo had told us about this being a good place to hunt. As time passed, it became just the rock. There were several fresh rubs in that area.

I sat on our new stand overlooking a small hemlock tree in the hollow below the game lands fields and saw two bears one morning. One looked to be about 150 pounds, but the other one was a huge old boar. We would have to sit someone on this stand for rifle bear season. As we name all of our stands, we decided to call this one the hollow stand.

The week of archery bear season found Larry and me in camp. While we saw no bears, we did see several deer. Friday evening, Crawford and Stan arrived in camp. Dave had sickness problems in his family with his wife and mother-in-law being ill with bronchitis, so he regrettably had to miss bear season this year. Saturday morning dawned crisp and cold, with temperatures in the twenties. Crawford decided to hunt at the good stand. I told Stan to sit at the hollow stand. Larry went to his ladder stand at the rock, and I went to the rock ledge overlooking Glade Run. Things got interesting shortly after seven o'clock when Stan spied a bear making his way uphill through the thicket below him. He took a shot at it through brush but missed, and the chase was on! As the bear accelerated to Mach 2 or so, Crawford touched off three rounds, rolling the bear on the third one. He reloaded and shot one more time, but the bear got up and took off again. We spent the rest of the morning following a decent blood trail across the road and down into the creek bottom for about a mile, emerging into Waley's soybean field.

The Waleys were cutting firewood and had seen the bear go across Jersey Hollow Road. Mrs. Waley told me that the bear came right up to their backyard. When it saw her, it veered uphill and crossed the cornfield next to Jersey Hollow Road. We decided to take a break in hopes that the bear would stop and lie down. Crawford and I resumed following the blood trail around eleven o'clock and went another mile or so into the game lands until we finally lost it. We hoped this bear would survive. (Update: Rick Steinmiller reported that some other hunters harvested the bear, a boar weighing 214 pounds. Apparently, Stan's shot grazed the boar's back and Crawford's hit the hind leg. Oh well. Progress was being made. At least we drew blood this year.)

Monday of rifle bear season was slow and wet. We saw a few deer and turkeys, but nobody was out hunting except for us. Crawford and Stan left for home Monday evening. The rest of bear season brought heavy rain, so Larry and I broke camp Tuesday morning and went home.

Dave and I returned to camp Friday evening after Thanksgiving. Saturday was spent hunting turkeys and putting up Dave's ladder stand in green briar hell. Sunday, we took a long look at the placement of Larry's ladder stand next to the laurel close to the rock. We made what turned out to be a super decision by deciding not to move it.

On Monday morning, with rain forecast for most of the day, we found out how accurate weather forecasts can be. It turned out to be mostly cloudy with only a few sprinkles. I sat in the hollow stand. Dave decided to go to his ladder stand above the food plots in green briar hell. Larry went to the rock stand. By 2:00, I had not seen a single deer, and neither had Larry, so he sent me a text asking, "Would you mind if I move to the good stand?" I told him I had no objection, and said, "Since I'm not seeing anything, do you mind if I move to yours?"

We each made the move described. By 4:00, I still had seen no deer. As I was sitting there thinking that this might be the first opening day of rifle season in which I had not seen even a single deer, I looked to my left and spied a doe walking slowly uphill through a thicket. As I watched, I noticed a buck following her. He appeared to be really big with a decent rack. When he presented me with a shot through brush, I took it. He moved off and stood broadside, so I shot again. He walked uphill and joined the doe. After ten minutes, I got down and found some blood, but the trail gave out before it crossed Harbaugh Road. I gave up and went back to the cabin. While there, Scott's dad and cousin showed up and asked if I could help Scott bring out his buck. It was a broken racked buck with four points on the left side. Dave saw a few deer, but nothing to shoot.

The next morning, Dave decided to go to the rocks at the corner of the game lands food plot. At nine o'clock, he called me on the radio and said he was going to push out the good cover on the ridge toward the condo where I was located. About half way there, he called back and told me he had found my buck. We managed to salvage a fair amount of meat from a huge eight-point, which we later made into bologna. I didn't feel very good about gut shooting one, but I guess those things happen from time to time, and I am not perfect. Later in the day, I put on a drive for Larry and moved some deer toward him, but he didn't see them.

On Wednesday, Larry decided to sleep in and give his cold a rest, so Dave went to his stand. I told Dave that I would leave the cabin about eight o'clock and put on a drive for him. I was part of the way through the drive when I contacted Dave on the radio to tell him I was coming and he should get ready. He replied that he had just shot a buck. I quit the drive and went to help him get his buck out of the woods.

Nothing much happened for the rest of the week. We put on drives for each other. Both Dave and Larry saw deer. Larry did have a chance on Thursday at a legal buck, but he wasn't able to determine it was legal until too late to take a shot. On Saturday morning, I put on a one-man drive through the laurel across the creek from our cabin and pushed out a group of ten deer with one buck in it. Dave took a shot at one of the does, but missed.

We packed up and winterized the camp on Sunday. All in all, this was a good year for us at Camp Rip-N-Tear. We took two does, two bucks (for the second straight year) and had shooting at a bear. Stan and Crawford got spring gobblers. I'll take a year like this anytime. Just to prove that we do have a few quality bucks in the area, here is a photo of Frank the Tank. Rick Steinmiller snapped this photo. A local hunter took him in the chestnut orchard on Scot Camp Road.

Frank the Tank

2012: Two Bucks And A Bear

As a side issue, January 2, 2012 brought tragedy to my other camp, Camp Bucktail. Mike Lloyd and his friend Travis Miller were there to hunt flintlock. While they were hunting, an overheated woodstove started a fire. Camp Bucktail was pretty much destroyed. During the coming weeks, the members dealt with insurance and decisions as to whether or not rebuilding was an option. At a cabin meeting Sunday, January 8, it was decided to rebuild. Spring and summer would be busy.

Dave stopped by our house early in the second week of January to deliver the bologna we got made from my buck. My share consisted of thirty-two one-pound sticks of the stuff, and it tasted really great. While he was there, we finalized plans to visit the cabin that weekend. Crawford and Stan were also planning on joining us for the final day of flintlock season. I thought I might stay part of the following week and try to see if there was a bobcat in the area since I had a bobcat tag.

That final week of flintlock season, nobody killed a deer. While opportunities presented themselves, for some reason or another, nobody dropped the hammer. Dave, who was sitting in Larry's stand at the rock, saw two bucks, but he had no buck tag. We filled feeders and set up a game camera on the one next to the cabin. Intentions were to split firewood, but we couldn't get the wood splitter started. Because it was so cold, perhaps the oil and hydraulic fluids had become too viscous.

Rick Sabo called me late in January and told me he was going to sell his twenty acres. He said he was asking $100,000 for it, which put it way out of our price range. I also had a phone conversation with Rick Steinmiller. He was now back to work and employed as an airframe maintenance specialist at an airport in Lynchburg, Virginia, so we probably would not be seeing him as often as we had. The weekend of February 12, I made the trek to camp to check on cameras and fill the feeders. There was a foot of snow, so I didn't walk down to the one in the hollow, but the feeder next to the cabin was empty. I put 300 pounds of corn into it. The camera was not aimed right. Most of the photos it took were just the heads of deer, but some were worth looking at. At least five different bucks and a dozen or so does were visiting this feeder. I adjusted the direction the camera was aimed so it would take better photos. Next, I noticed that the wood splitter had a flat tire. After pumping it up, I got the motor running with a squirt of starting fluid. It now worked fine, so I split a fair amount of wood.

Dave and I went to the cabin the last weekend of February to fill the feeders and take down stands. We got two of the stands on state game lands removed and put into the shed. The upper feeder was empty, so we put 300 pounds of corn and oats into it. The feeder was apparently being visited by a number of hungry animals. The wood splitter tire was flat again. We tried unsuccessfully to take the wheel off, intending to get it repaired at a tire shop. Another plan for this had to be formulated.

Back at Camp Bucktail, work was progressing on site preparation for a new camp. John Bartholow and I managed to get most of the necessary trees cut for the excavator to come in and prepare a site for the new Camp Bucktail. Will and Mike Lloyd, their cousin Ian, and a couple of other young strong backs put most of the remains of the cabin into a rollback dumpster on Sunday, March 4, and it was hauled away to a landfill.

I had intended to go to Camp Rip-N-Tear the weekend of March 9-12, but while doing some chainsaw work at Camp Bucktail, I fell and tore tendons in my left shoulder. A visit to my favorite orthopedist, Dr. Bruno, ended with me being referred to his colleague, Dr. Tom, who is an expert in that area. Surgery was scheduled for April 5, thus putting a damper on my spring hunting and fishing. Larry returned home from a vacation in Florida that weekend, so we went out and filled the feeders on Thursday, March 22. While there, we implemented plan B, which involved using Fix-A-Flat to inflate that wood splitter tire. Of course, due to my infirmity, Larry did most of the work. Plan B succeeded, and the wood splitter once again had a round tire.

Surgery took place as scheduled on April 5. I was facing six weeks of doing nothing substantial. Larry and Dave went to the cabin the weekend of April 13 to fill the feeders and download photos from the game cameras. By that weekend, all of the bucks had lost last year's antlers. The photos revealed that we had a resident bear, a couple of boss gobblers, and the usual retinue of deer.

The first week of May, Larry, Dave, and I visited the cabin with the intention of splitting some firewood and for them to get in some turkey hunting while I continued to recuperate. I guess one out of two isn't bad. The best day of turkey hunting was Thursday morning when, during a thunderstorm, the jakes and gobblers were really sounding off. None came in to the guys' calls, however. The wood splitter still gave us fits. It would fire up and quit running immediately. My suspicion was that the carburetor got gummed up, and I would have to either replace the wood splitter or get it repaired again. After a rain on Wednesday, we decided to say goodbye to the man-eating recliner that came with the cabin. Larry donated a Lazy Boy rocker/recliner that he thought would be much better. The man-eating chair made a cheery fire.

Over Memorial Day weekend, Crawford, Karen, Nathan, and Seth were in camp. As usual, the boys had a great time exploring the area and building a dam in Drake Run. Karen spent a lot of the time resting. Most of the weekend was uneventful, but while running the six-wheeler in the hollow, Crawford injured his back as he was moving a tree out of the way. His weekend work was done.

I went out to the cabin the following weekend. Rick Steinmiller and his family invited me to a cookout, which was pretty nice. Chad and Rick helped me get the wood splitter out of the shed. I worked on it, but whatever was wrong was beyond my ability to fix, so Chad and I took it to Confluence Hardware where the repairman in the basement could work his magic on it when he got time. My intention was to return to the cabin when it was done and put it to work. While there, I downloaded a few photos from the game cameras. Both feeders were empty. Since I had no corn, they stayed that way.

Friday, June 15, I visited the cabin to bail the wood splitter out of Confluence Hardware's repair shop. I was successful in that endeavor. The wood splitter had a new carburetor and was back to functioning the way wood splitters are supposed to. It ran and split wood. While at camp, I posted some of the new aluminum no trespassing signs along our property line with the state game lands. I finished the job later in June, and the perimeter of the property was now completely posted. I also downloaded photos from the game camera. The same bear seemed to be visiting occasionally, so we had at least one in the area. While I was sitting on the porch early Sunday morning, a doe with twin fawns came in to the feeder. These were the first fawns I had seen that summer. One photo showed two does fighting. They stood up on their hind legs and got into what might best be described as a boxing match. Unfortunately, the photo was of poor quality (I got a much better photo of this behavior in 2016).

Two does fighting

The second weekend in July, Larry and I went out to the cabin to put some corn in the feeder since I would be in the Smoky Mountains on vacation with the family the next week. I also towed my trailer and Kubota tractor out to grade the driveway. We went to the Dogwood Acres restaurant for dinner Thursday evening. On the way back, I noticed that the truck had squishy brakes, so I went to Hartman's service station in Confluence to see if I could get my brakes fixed. The mechanic there couldn't help me, but we managed to fill up the brake fluid reservoir with brake fluid purchased at Dollar General and limped home. We left the tractor and trailer at the cabin. That turned out to be a good thing since it rained really hard the following Friday. It was already there to regrade the driveway. After I returned home from vacation, Larry and I made a midweek trip out to the cabin to fill the feeder and put out some salt blocks. I graded the driveway one more time and then took my tractor home.

On Friday, August 3, I received a check from Camp Bucktail as payment for my share of that camp. Henceforth, I planned to spend all of my PA hunting time here at Camp Rip-N-Tear. I decided to make the drive to camp to fill the feeder and download photos. The feeder apparently had been quite busy, as it was just about empty. I put 200 pounds of corn in it and planned to come out the next week with Dave and Larry to fill it again. Also, the SD card from the camera had over 800 photos on it taken during that short time.

We made several other weekend trips in August. By the end of that month, it was time to start putting out stands. The first ones to go up were those on our property. During September, we erected the rest. This gave the deer a chance to get used to them being there. My shoulder had recovered enough that I could use the log splitter to split some of the smaller logs. I also dumped two buckets of apples Doris and I picked from our wild apple tree at home. It seemed that the deer really liked them.

Tragedy struck the Steinmiller camp toward the end of September. Craig Sabo's son Steven came up the driveway one day while Larry and I were resting from our labors. He told us that he and his father were at Rick's cabin and that it had been broken into. Thieves stole some guns and a chainsaw. They also damaged Rick's plumbing system by removing the copper pipes. This just reinforces my belief that one should not leave anything in a cabin that he does not want to lose to thieves. It is a shame, but not all people are good people. There is probably no way to make a cabin break-in proof. We are lucky in that our camp is located some distance from the road. Thieves and vandals would have to walk uphill and carry their stolen items out. Most thieves are not that ambitious. Still, it makes no sense to leave expensive items in a cabin that will not be occupied much of the time.

September 29 ushered in the start of archery deer season, and Larry and I answered the call to arms. Larry opened the scoring with a nice doe taken on the first Monday while hunting out of his stand along the Glade Run hollow. We did not see many deer that week, but I did have an opportunity to harvest a doe which I decided not to take. I saw only seven deer the entire week and Larry a few less. This was to be the only hunting we would do early in the season as I was scheduled again to go to South Carolina's Deerfield Plantation the third week of October. While there, I took two does and a six-point. The freezer was now replenished.

On October 29, a fierce lady named Sandy paid us a visit in Saint Thomas. I spent the next nine days cleaning up and repairing storm damage. This seriously cut into my hunting time. During the storm, severe wind uprooted two large white pine trees. They went down with a crash in our front yard as Doris watched. In addition, we lost over fifty other trees on our property. These needed to be cut up for either firewood or pulpwood. The roof blew off our hay barn. (Son Kenneth and his friend Lorenzo had helped me build this barn during the 1970s when both of them were teenagers.) Cutting firewood and ranking pulpwood to take to a paper mill, along with various other repairs, got done during that time.

Doris loads hay from a badly damaged hay barn.

While I was otherwise occupied with Sandy cleanup, Dave and Larry went out to check on camp the weekend of November 3. Power was off for most of the week. They hooked up Rick Steinmiller's generator, ran the refrigerator for awhile, and then watched television using power from the same. The electricity went back on Saturday night while they slept. There were lots of downed limbs and a few dead trees for us to cut up and add to the firewood pile.

Finally, the cleanup work was under control. Larry and I returned to camp November 7. We discussed strategy, and Larry decided to go to the stand I had put up at the head of the hollow below the first game lands food plot. Around 10:00 AM, he saw a doe and twin fawns, followed by a smaller buck he was not sure would be legal. Shortly after that, a really nice eight-point came along. While he had to shoot through a very narrow window in the brush, his bolt flew true. When he got back to camp, he told a five-minute tale which finally ended with him having a buck down. We returned to the kill site and took the following photo before hauling it to camp.

Thursday evening, Dave joined us at camp. He had decided to take a day off from work and do some hunting with his crossbow. Larry drove home Friday to drop his buck off at Darrel Grove's butcher shop in Saint Thomas. That morning, Dave made his first crossbow kill, taking a smallish sort of doe from his new deer blind along the hollow to the southwest of the game lands fields.

Larry, with "Lefty," the best buck taken up to that time at Camp Rip-N-Tear.

On Saturday, I hunted out of the good stand and had two bucks go past. I took a shot at the largest, an eight-point, but did not make a good one. We spent most of the morning following his blood trail for more than a mile, but it finally gave out. While returning to camp, Dave and I jumped another buck that appeared to be either a six or eight-point. As the distance to him was well beyond ethical shooting range, no shot was taken.

Dave's Veterans Day seven-point

Dave and I worked most of Sunday morning cutting up downed wood from Sandy. We were prepared for the guys to have some fun splitting wood during bear season. We also put up a new ladder stand in the hollow below camp across Drake Run along the old logging road. Larry returned that afternoon.

Monday was a very unusual day in that archery deer season had been extended to include the observed Veterans Day holiday. Archery bear season began on the same day. Dave started the day in the new stand we had erected the day before. At 7:05 AM, a nice yearling seven-point walked past and gave him a standing broadside shot. Dave had his second bow kill in two hunting days.

We spent the rest of the morning processing his kill, and he loaded up his truck for the trip home shortly after noon. That left Larry and me to hunt bear for the rest of the day. The wind came up and trees were falling. Since being in the woods was dangerous, we cut our afternoon hunt short. I drove home to check on Doris and take care of a few chores, leaving Larry in charge of camp and the TV remote, and planned to fix what wasn't working when I got back.

I returned to camp Tuesday evening, November13. Shortly after I arrived, Larry came back from the day's hunt with an interesting story. It seemed that he had a bear in the vicinity of the blowdown stand for over seven hours, but never had a clear shot. He left the woods, thinking that with the crossbow he would have only one shot and the bear might attack if wounded. We discussed his experiences of the day for awhile and decided that the next morning I would set up in the ladder stand at the end of the stone ridge, and he would return to the blowdown stand.

Wednesday morning, we left camp before dawn and hiked to our chosen ladder stands. On the way, Larry told me that a deer passed his stand first, and at 8:45, the bear arrived. Almost exactly the same thing happened again! First a couple of does passed in the thick stuff below him, and since archery deer season had ended, he could not take one of them. Then at 8:45, the bear appeared. This time it did things a little differently, passing him at a range of about sixty yards, too far for an ethical shot, then crossing the road and the ridge above it before going out of his sight.

Ten minutes later, not having known of any of this, I looked down the hillside below me and spied a bear walking at an angle uphill that would take it past me at a distance of about twenty-five yards. I picked an opening between two saplings. When the bear entered that space, I squeezed the trigger, thus sending a bolt on its way. The shot was true, and the bear went downhill for a short distance, perhaps forty yards. It disappeared behind a brush pile. I waited the required fifteen minutes and then yelled, "Larry, get over here!"

The author and the crossbow bear

As Larry approached, I told him that I had taken a shot and thought I had a bear down. Sure enough, the bear lay behind that brushpile. The first bear kill for Camp Rip-N-Tear was now history. The two of us brought the bear back to camp and hung it up on the tripod. We took two hero shots, one with me and another with Larry, since he discovered the location and was the key to this success.

We then loaded the bear into my truck, and I drove to meet a game warden to report my kill and to get it tagged. I left immediately from there to take the bear to my taxidermist. Mac skinned it and cut it into two halves for me. I returned to camp that evening for the celebration. Since only the two of us were in camp, I regret that Dave and Crawford were not present to participate in the festivities.

The next day I set about butchering the bear while Larry continued to hunt. The amount of fat all over the carcass was incredible. In some places, it was over an inch thick. I removed the edible meat and got several roasts out of it to cook later, ground up much of the rest into burger, and saved a bunch of chopped meat to make a stew for camp. The stew was wonderful.

Rifle bear season came in on Saturday, November 17, and saw Crawford, Larry, Dave, and me in camp. Stan had to work, so he missed out on the fun. Sunday, I prepared a large kettle of bear stew/soup, and the guys allowed as how it was pretty fair. On Monday, by request, I did the recipe with deer tenderloin, celery and mushroom soup, potatoes, and carrots. As usual, there were no leftovers.

Unfortunately, it seemed that I had killed the only bear in our area during archery season, as no bears were sighted during the two days we hunted, nor was much shooting heard. The local gangs did not drive, which led us to believe that they hunted elsewhere. A spotty acorn crop probably caused the bigger bears to move elsewhere in search of food. This year, bear season opened as early as it ever will, with Thanksgiving being on November 22. Next year, everything would be moved back a week, and perhaps the weather might be somewhat colder.

After spending Thanksgiving with the family, I returned to camp on Saturday to find Dave already there. We set about getting the cabin warm and fired up the wood splitter. After finishing that chore, we figured we had enough split wood to take care of our needs for the next two years or so. Dave intended to hunt on Mount Davis to fill his DMAP tag. I was the only hunter who pursued deer here for the first four days of rifle deer season. Pursue them, I did. Larry was also in camp, but as he already had harvested a buck, he served as camp cook. He brought two gallons of vegetable soup for us to munch on, and it served adequately in that capacity.

Lefty and Righty: One can see the difference in brow tines.

Monday, I decided to use Larry's stand, the one from which Dave and I both killed eight-points during the first week of last year's rifle season. At 8:00 AM, I did see three deer, but the wind was wrong. They got a whiff of me and departed the area. One of them was the buck we call "Righty," so named because his right brow tine was longer than his left brow tine. We determined this from game camera photos. Larry's eight-point was named "Lefty" because his left side brow tine was longer. Other than that, the two bucks might have been twins.

Tuesday, I hunted on the blowdown stand. In the morning, I did see a pair of does that walked within ten feet of the base of the ladder stand and never made me. That evening, close to 5:00 PM, I watched seven does and one four-point pass to my left. Try as I might, I could not put a brow tine on the four-point.

Dave reported that he was not seeing shooter does on Mount Davis, but on Tuesday he did see a quality buck that would have been a shooter if he had not already used his buck tag. He also reported that the weather was much colder on the big mountain, and there was a decent amount of snow, nothing unusual for Mount Davis in December.

Wednesday, I hunted the brown stand in the morning and what we now were calling the bear stand (so named due to my taking that bear from it during archery season) that evening. I did not see any deer all day.

Thursday morning, I tried the rock stand since the wind had changed to a more favorable direction. Again, I did not see any deer. That evening, I decided to give Dave's pop-up blind a try and did see two does. They would not be legal for another few days, so I remained deerless for the season. Dave was still not making the connections he needed on the big mountain. He reported that the sign was there, but very few hunters were moving the deer, in which case hunting can be difficult. That evening Crawford arrived with grandson Seth for his first hunt out of the cabin. I suggested that they hunt the hollow stand or the good stand, since neither had been used so far.

Friday morning, they hunted out of a ground blind near the hemlock tree close to the hollow stand and saw five does. They returned that evening and saw four more. Meanwhile I hunted the bear stand in the morning and saw no deer. That evening I hiked uphill to the brown ladder stand. This stand was, and still is, an evening stand. I saw five deer, one of which was a four-point that rubbed a small sapling as I watched. The deer came out just as the sun was setting. I waited until dark and then made the familiar hike back to camp.

Saturday morning saw Crawford and Seth in the ground blind at the hollow stand and me in Dave's ladder stand along the creek bottom road. While they saw close to ten deer, and does were legal game, Seth did not take a shot. I am not certain why he did not, but perhaps he did not have an opening or the deer were too far away. I saw no deer that morning. Evening would be different for us. I hiked to the brown ladder stand again. Crawford and Seth set up in Dave's pop-up blind. At 4:40 PM, a group of six deer approached my stand. One old doe saw me sitting there. She snorted, and a Chinese fire drill ensued where I had only one shot that was makeable. I took an antlerless deer that turned out to be a button buck. Crawford and Seth saw eight or more deer. Those made their way uphill toward the brown ladder. If I had been in it at the time, I may have had a chance at "Righty" who was among that group. By then, I was dragging my deer out to await them at the old oak tree. Crawford dragged my deer out for me. It may have been "be nice to old guys" day.

On Sunday December 2, we did a few chores such as setting up the feeder in the hollow and filling both it and the gravity feeder at the cabin. Crawford also installed a ladder at the box blind next to the sand mound. We left to go home about 11:00 AM.

One more season was in the books for Camp Rip-N-Tear. It had been the most successful yet for us. We took two bucks, three antlerless deer, and a bear (our first since we began hunting here). I did have a chance at a buck, but blew it, or it may have been an even better season. It would have been really nice if Seth had been able to get a deer.

Since grandson Seth had taken a day off from school to go hunting with Dad and Grandpa, his assignment was to write a short essay about his experience in camp and what he had learned. What follows is his essay.

Seth's visit to Camp Rip-N-Tear

I learned many different things on my hunting trip. I've learned many things in hunting season, but my dad normally finds the deer. This year I found many deer, but I didn't get to shoot any. I've learned that hunting is in no way easy. You have to have lots of patience and aim and also you have to be able to stay calm when you spot a deer. My grandpa shot a deer and no one else did, actually. It was a small deer with small antlers, almost no antlers actually, but it was worth shooting to him. I have always liked hunting, particularly because I get to hang out with family while doing something that is just plain fun for me to do. Not all of my family hunts though, actually now that I think about it, barely any of my family hunts or even my friends. Hunting can be very hard, especially for me since I am not very patient, calm, or even quiet, but somehow, I have been doing pretty well when hunting. I guess you could say hunting is making me a little bit more mature than I used to be. I have definitely learned a lot.

2013: Lucky Thirteen

Shortly after New Year's Day, Crawford, Dave, and I went to camp for a few days to do some flintlock hunting. This has become a tradition with us, and while no deer were taken (as usual), we each saw deer every day. Crawford actually harvested a tree that got in the way. He watched a bachelor group of five bucks go past his stand (Of course he did not have a buck tag.) and we all saw numerous does. With the snow and cold temperatures being common in January, flintlock hunting is always tough. By the time this late season rolls around, the deer have been through close to three months of hunting pressure, and they are always extremely wary. No matter, as we always have fun doing it.

Before leaving camp, we filled the feeders and put fresh batteries in the cameras. According to the photos we got from the cameras since the end of rifle deer season, some really nice bucks survived. They had only one more week until the dangerous time was over. Then they would have something different to worry about. Winter is the mean season for them. Meals are hard to come by, and they must eat enough to produce heat and avoid freezing. Deer are tough animals though. I have not found a winter-killed deer in years.

As our Pennsylvania Game Commission now requires that we have our ladder stands removed from the state game lands during the off season, Dave, Larry, and I finally made it to camp the second weekend of February. Due to the forecast of bad weather, including freezing rain for Friday, we arrived Thursday evening. We immediately stoked the woodstove. It would take about four hours to warm up the cabin from a starting temperature in the twenties. Friday morning, we removed tree stands to be hauled to the shed for winter storage. We finished the job before noon. That was a good thing because it started to rain as the last stand went into the shed.

The weather changed overnight. Saturday morning dawned with the temperature in the teens and light snow falling. Dave pronounced that this would be a good day to cut some wood. Larry and Dave went down the driveway to where the big red oak had fallen two years previously. I cut up some of the standing dead white oak closer to the cabin. In fairly short order we had both pickups loaded with some fine quality firewood. Dave and Larry then carried a salt block up to a place above the second game lands food plot where Larry wanted to put a stand. Unfortunately, Larry overdid it. He spent a painful night, so we cleaned up and left for home Sunday morning.

On a Thursday, two weeks later, I drove to camp. It was very cold when I arrived. Again, it would take four hours to get the cabin warm with just the woodstove, so I put a large pot of venison vegetable soup on the stove and then took a walk to do inventory. Snow depth at the cabin (1941 feet above sea level at the front lawn) was a couple inches of crusty and crunchy stuff, but upon gaining elevation, it got deeper. The north facing slopes still had about a foot or more, and that made hiking on the hillsides challenging. As usual, the tracks in the snow told a story. A fairly large pack of coyotes had made the rounds. There were plenty of deer tracks, and a number of turkeys scratched the forest floor for a living. The absence of bear tracks in the snow indicated that all of our resident bears were sleeping off the gluttony of the past year.

Remains of the Harbaugh homestead are located on a hillside below the game lands fields. This family had built a home during the first decades of the twentieth century, cleared some land, and mined coal for their own use. What remains of the homestead is a stone foundation and an old wooden privy, part of which still stands. There is an old trash dump that I intend to explore someday to look for old bottles, but for various reasons, never seem to get around to doing so. The Pennsylvania Game Commission acquired this land during the great depression. They have kept the Harbaugh fields from reverting to woods by mowing it once a year, but only weedy growth persists. A few years ago, I volunteered to bring my tractor and equipment there to till and plant a good food plot. The land manager refused my offer, but said that if I wanted to pay for his guys to do it, he would accept that. I decided I did not want to spend that much more than it would have cost me to do the work myself, so I withdrew the offer.

Traipsing through the area, I noted evidence of heavy deer travel. We had a ladder stand nearby where Larry got the nice eight-point last fall. The area close to where it was located had been heavily used. I continued on downhill to a logging path that parallels the creek and then forded it to investigate some laurel thickets to the north.

Most of the deer beds I encountered were clustered under hemlock trees, probably so deer could find shelter from winter wind and precipitation.

It was amazing how their numbers had recovered in the area. I crossed the creek one more time and climbed the hill to camp. Upon returning, the inside temperature had risen to nearly 50°. I sampled the soup, which by the way tasted pretty decent. The weather comedian was now forecasting light wintery mix for the morning.

Dave arrived on the scene about mid-morning the next day. We decided to take another walk, this time below the road and across the swamp. Many more deer, turkey, and coyote tracks were seen in that area. It was becoming obvious to me that a trip to camp with the shotgun might be in order with the aim of harvesting a coyote for my trophy room (jokingly called the museum).

It seems that I am always learning something. I guess when that stops, I will be in the next plane of existence. What I may have learned about our local deer on this winter inventory trip is that their winter travel routes are quite different from those of fall. During fall, most of the deer sign is close to the fields and Back Road. During winter, much of that sign is gone, and there is more deer activity deeper in the woods. I wonder if this is because what they are eating changes with the seasons or because recent hunter activity pushed them away from easily accessible woodland. I suspect it is the former, since a deer's wintertime diet is mostly browse.

Saturday evening, a couple of guys who own a neighboring camp, Joe and Mark Giovannitti, showed up, and we swapped lies. The temperature on Saturday afternoon had risen into the fifties, and much of the snow melted. It was so nice out that Dave and I actually sat on the porch with a cigar and a beer. Life is tough, but someone has to do the hard jobs.

Most of March was taken up by trying to keep warm and planning revenge on Punxsutawney Phil for such a messed-up forecast. He predicted an early spring, and that was far from the case. At the end of March, the PA Cross Country Skiers Association (http://www.paccsa.org/lrwebcam) webcam picture still showed over a foot of snow in the Laurel Highlands. By the beginning of April, weather had improved somewhat. The ground finally thawed, so Doris and I set about repairing some fences around our pasture at home. Nick Sabetto supplied us with a bunch of rocks. We used them to rock in the new fence posts. Let me tell you that rocking in fence posts is not as much fun as it used to be.

Larry's project for the spring was to plant some apple trees. We picked them up at an Adams County nursery the second week of April and then drove out to camp. Planting the trees involved digging holes with a digging iron and a spade. This is actually work. We placed them in locations along the sewer line and around the storage shed. Along with these trees, I added two wild apple trees that came up along our fence row at home. We would need to be wary of bear damage.

Unfortunately, we discovered another problem when we turned the water system back on. We had a leak in one line that led to the shower. It was inside a paneled wall between the living room and bathroom. The leak soaked the carpeting. After turning off the water, I called Confluence Hardware. They promised to send us a plumber on Monday morning. Their plumber, Stephanie, arrived as promised on Monday to fix the water system. It took her and her helper about half an hour to replace the leaking couplings. After that, we pressurized the water system and checked for leaks. This ended our problem, but we must more careful in draining the water system in the future when we winterize the cabin. To this end, I purchased an air compressor so we can blow out the lines.

I also made arrangements with Stephanie to do the installation of an iron filter the following week. Water from our well contains a lot of iron. This caused the water to be very hard and put a reddish deposit on all of our plumbing fixtures. We purchased an iron filter from Home Depot (the Water Boss Iron Reduction Filter, model 900if). Having water without a ton of iron in it certainly has made the cabin a whole lot more livable. The filter takes out most of the iron, but not 100%. The iron filter uses a resin which is regenerated by flushing it with potassium permanganate solution as needed. We know more of this solution is needed when the water becomes slightly red orange in color.

Crawford and I spent Saturday, April 27, pursuing the wily turkey gobblers that live in the area. We started the morning with some turks gobbling near Rick Steinmiller's cabin. I evidently got a bit too close and spooked them off the roost, but they flew directly toward Crawford. Crawford said that if he sets up in the hollow along the creek, the birds go toward the top of the hill, and vice versa. It worked out that way for him, as usual. Later in the morning, he had a chance at a gobbler close to Craig's wooden stand. Chance is all it was though. He did not see the bird until it had already seen him.

The first weekend in May, Crawford and I returned to camp. We arose Saturday morning and had a cup of coffee on the porch, waiting for the first gobbler to sound off. Shortly after 5:30, it happened. One gobbled less than 100 yards from the cabin in the hollow, so Crawford went that way. I took off up the road into the game lands and set up by the dead white oak stump in sight of the food plot tree stand. As dawn broke, I spied a dark object making its way uphill. My initial thought was a gobbler responding to my calls, but as it got closer, it turned out to be a smaller black bear which crossed the road a short distance from me. Shortly, two bucks ambled by, each already growing his new antlers. Back at camp later in the morning, we saw nine does from the porch. All in all, this turned out to be a great morning. Crawford left for home soon after noon on Saturday. Later in the day, I went fishing on Laurel Hill Creek and found a hatch in progress, so I tied on a light Cahill pattern dry fly and managed to catch and release several brown trout.

Sunday morning, I got up late with the intention of going into town for brunch, but when I tried starting my Chevy truck, it did not cooperate. It would start and then seemed to run out of gas and shut off, so I called AAA to come and haul the truck home. I resolved that this would be the end of the Chevy. Strangely enough, after I set up the service call, I tried to start the truck. This time it ran. I called AAA to cancel their service call and decided to drive home. No problems on the way home, but on Monday we ventured out to check prices. Jennings Chevrolet in Chambersburg gave us a price on a new heavy duty work truck with an eight-foot bed that we could not refuse. We signed the papers and made arrangements to have the cap transferred and the bed coated with Rhino lining.

I returned to camp the second weekend in May. This time I got there very late Thursday morning and decided to go trout fishing since Laurel Hill Creek had been stocked earlier in the day. I thought I might hang a trout or two for dinner. It is great when a plan works out. I caught and released a bunch of trout, keeping one decent rainbow for the grill. The pattern that worked like a charm was a black wooly bugger. The woods were quiet when I returned to camp. I wondered when cicadas would emerge. The news on Channel 6 out of Johnstown said that this should be the year. Then the quiet would surely end.

Things got a bit on the exciting side when six deer came in to the corn pile next to the cabin food plot. After feeding for ten minutes or so, they took off, snorting as they ran. The cause of that was a sow bear who showed up with three yearling cubs. She and the cubs fed for quite some time before they departed, traveling on the path toward Craig's wooden stand.

Friday morning, I left the cabin long before dawn started to stain the horizon and set up at the blowdown. At first light, a gobbler sounded off downhill from me, probably roosting in the hemlock grove along the creek at the bottom of the hill. I did a few tree cluck/yelps, and he went ballistic! I figured I had one on the string. Well, in the never-ending saga of what could go wrong, something of course did go wrong. He was on his way to me. I saw him go into a strut just out of range, but he suddenly did an alarm putt and took off flying. I wondered what I did wrong, but it wasn't me that did it. The same young bear I saw last week emerged from the thick stuff right where the gobbler had taken off. This had never happened to me. Was the bear also turkey hunting?

The Channel 6 weather comedian said rain would be arriving sometime during the morning, and it did, along with some thunder. The wind kicked up during the thunderstorm, causing me to beat feet it back to the cabin. I dislike being pelted by rain, but I dislike trees falling on me even more. It rained off and on for the rest of the day with some of the rain falling pretty heavily. Rain continued for most of the night and into Saturday morning. The decision was made that hunting turkeys would not be the order of that day. As I get older, I no longer have the desire to hunt when I am wet and cold. I guess this is a failing of sorts. It is what it is, or as Popeye would say, "I yam what I yam." I spent much of the day reading and watching TV, returning home on Sunday.

After completing the honeydo chores of the day, I decided to return to camp the following Wednesday. Arriving late in the afternoon, I replenished the corn supply and downloaded photos from the trail camera. It appeared that the deer had split up to have their fawns because the group of seven that had been regulars was now a group of three. The bears were still making use of the corn pile. One was a decent sized boar.

I hunted turkeys Thursday and Friday morning. Not a single turkey sounded off. Crawford arrived Friday afternoon. We sat on the porch listening for gobbles, but the only sound we heard was woodpeckers drumming on trees. The breeding season seemed to be over. I left to come home Saturday afternoon. Crawford stayed until Sunday.

I made several weekend visits to the cabin in June, mostly to replenish the corn pile we had out near the food plot to the west of the cabin. During each visit, I saw bears at the corn pile and also downloaded photos from the trail camera overlooking it. From some of the photos, it became clear that the sows had kicked out their yearling cubs and were preparing for the breeding season. One of the most exciting times in the history of our camp happened shortly after 4:00 PM on June 15 when a huge boar and a smaller sow came in. The boar was obviously after the sow and waiting for her to come into heat, but she was not ready. He would attempt to mount her, but she would growl at him and pull away. He got high grades for persistence. I managed to get a few photos while standing on the porch, but the trail camera malfunctioned and took none. In the photo below you can see the boar in pursuit of the sow.

Mating season begins.

The third weekend in June, Larry and I journeyed to camp. I got there first and spent some time on Friday restocking the corn pile and downloading photos from the game camera. As near as I could tell, we had at least five and probably more different bears coming in for corn. Larry arrived shortly, and we watched a small bear feeding. Saturday morning, we watched a couple of bears and a deer at the feeder before firing up the chainsaw to cut some firewood. A problem arose when I tried to start the six-wheeler. It started, but put out a huge amount of smoke. This would certainly require Crawford's attention. We carried most of the wood to the fire pit area to finish cutting and filled out the low spots on the porch.

On Sunday morning, another boar and sow sauntered in just as dawn arose. They stayed for quite awhile. Apparently, this sow was also not ready to breed. After they left, another smaller bear approached, but lay down next to the rifle range target. We suspected that he smelled the big boar and was afraid to come closer.

The weekend of July 13, Doris and I went the cabin to beat the heat. We took our son's dogs (which we call Oofie Woofs) along. They were visiting us for doggie camp. While unloading the truck, I jumped up and hit my head on the top of the cap, sustaining a cut in my scalp that bled like all get out. We did stay overnight, but I needed some medical attention, so we left early on Sunday morning. The nice folks at Med Express put in a few staples. I hoped to be as good as new after it healed.

Is this love, or what?

Doris and I again took the Oofie Woofs to camp the first weekend of August. We went for a walk along Back Road toward the Steinmiller Camp and found Jimmy Yancy and his family in residence. Jimmy is Uncle Al's son-in-law. His wife, Al's daughter, is an elementary school teacher, so she and Doris had something in common. Jimmy expressed interest in having a camp himself. The land in this area surely is expensive. Rick Sabo sold his twenty acres that sits across Back Road from the Steinmiller Camp for a high price while keeping the mineral rights. Since we are located in an area that is above coal deposits and the two shale gas layers (Marcellus and Utica), our mineral rights may be worth something someday.

A lot of rain fell during August. The woods were greener than I could ever remember, giving me hope that the acorn crop might be good this year. A neighbor, Janet Waley, told me that we had over two inches of rain on August 22. The creeks and rivers were running bank full and muddy that weekend.

Labor Day weekend found Crawford and me in camp. Our chores included fixing the six-wheeler, adding a three-foot piece of chimney pipe to the chimney so the woodstove would have better draft, and setting up a few treestands. We put one tree stand up in the hollow close to where Larry shot the big eight-point last fall. It was a double wide stand, so Crawford and Seth would have first dibs on it during rifle season. We also set the bear stand (so named because I shot the bear there last year) and its counterpart (the blowdown stand) across the road. The feeder was empty, and we brought no corn to fill it, so we did not expect to see much wildlife around camp. Plenty of natural food was available for the critters.

Dave and I visited camp the second weekend of September, arriving that Friday evening. We spent most of the time putting up stands and replacing the ratcheting tie straps that hold them to the trees.

Monday morning arrived with rain. Dave walked to the game lands food plots to check a mineral lick he had put out during the winter. Upon returning, he reported that the game commission employees had finally cleared downed trees that had blocked the road after hurricane Sandy. This opened Harbaugh Road from the Jersey Hollow Road parking lot. As usual, they mowed only the edges of the food plot. As this plot is a mile from that parking lot, we couldn't understand why they would drive a tractor so far and not mow the entire plot. Because of the inclement weather, we decided to head for home a bit earlier in the day than planned.

It was getting closer to the opening of archery deer season, so I wanted to be in camp the last weekend of September. After arriving Friday afternoon, I did a few last-minute chores such as taking the chainsaw to the old logging road in the hollow and finishing the cut through the huge tree that fell across it. I did make three cuts in the trunk, but could not move the logs. This required Dave's assistance and some tools such as a digging iron and a cant hook to move them. The logs were about three feet in diameter. Once the logs were removed, it became possible to take the six-wheeler all the way to the good stand. On Saturday, I also hauled some firewood to Rick Steinmiller's cabin so his folks could stay warm. Just being neighborly, I guess.

The opener of archery deer season drew nigh with Dave and me in camp on Friday, October 4. Hopes were high, even though we had not seen or photographed any bucks since winter released its icy grip. The two of us hunted on Saturday, both morning and evening. I tried the front stand in the morning and the rock stand that evening. Dave sat on the bear stand in the morning and the food plot stand that afternoon. The temperature hovered in the eighties. Deer were just not moving, so neither of us saw anything. Monday morning brought a driving rain that preceded a cold front. When the rain stopped, the temperature began to drop. Because Dave had to work on Tuesday, he took off for home early in the afternoon. That evening I sat on the blowdown stand until it was almost too dark to see, but no deer passed by.

On Tuesday morning, I hiked to the new hollow stand, a comfortable two-man Big Dog stand that replaces the mostly uncomfortable bargain stand we had there last year. It proved to be just as unproductive with only a few chipmunks to break the monotony. Since the deer were not being very cooperative, I decided to return home that afternoon to do my wash in preparation for my upcoming South Carolina trip with Crawford and Seth.

Lucky 2013 was turning out to be not so lucky, for me at least. For the first time ever, I returned home from South Carolina with no deer. I saw only one deer on all of the stands. Seth had better luck, taking a nice doe. At least the Peters family would be able to eat. The Naugle freezer was getting empty.

The third week of October, early muzzleloader season, I hunted that Tuesday and Wednesday. While carrying the inline muzzleloader, I saw several bucks which were not legal unless one was archery hunting. I did not see any does to shoot. Dave arrived Thursday afternoon. On Friday morning, we drove to Mount Davis to hunt the DMAP. With snow falling apace, I took a stand above the hollow along Camp Bucky Road while Dave climbed the hill across the road from me. During a lull in the snowstorm, I spied three deer making their way parallel to the road on the other side of the hollow but could not get a shot at any of them. We returned to camp once again without a deer from the DMAP area.

Friday evening, Crawford and Seth joined us in camp. Crawford decided to take Seth to the hollow two-man stand. Dave hiked to the brown ladder stand on the edge of the oak flat above the game lands food plots. I opted to hunt the good stand. Around 8:00 AM, I heard a total of four shots that sounded like they might have come from the area the guys were hunting. Fifteen minutes later, I heard a single shot that sounded somewhat farther away. I saw no deer that morning, but the scrape close to the good stand obviously had been freshened the night before, so at least one buck was frequenting the hollow below camp.

I returned to camp about 10:30 and found Crawford getting the six-wheeler ready to travel. Seth had shot a big doe, but Crawford had forgotten to take a knife to gut it. I went with him to help retrieve it. Seth had shot the doe from a large group of deer that came up the hollow. Actually, there were two groups; one of seven or eight and the other with three. The group of three continued on toward Dave's stand. That had been the single shot I heard earlier. Seth's doe was a big one. Crawford and I had a tough drag to get it to where we could load it on to the six-wheeler.

As we finished the drag, I heard Dave on the road above us. We loaded both deer and proceeded back to camp for a skinning party. I used the PGC's chest tape to estimate their weight. To my amazement Dave's doe weighed close to 170 pounds dressed while Seth's came in at 140 pounds. Both deer were larger than many bucks I have taken over the years. No additional deer were killed during the week, but the rut was starting to kick in. Dave reported seeing scrapes along the edge of the second PGC food plot.

I returned to camp on Tuesday, October 29, hoping to improve my luck, which had been on the "snake bit" side this year so far. That evening, I hiked to the rock stand and did not see any deer, but two ruffed grouse showed up. At least I was seeing game.

On Wednesday morning, rains and wind hit in full force. The power went off sometime before 5:00 AM and with high winds, I decided not to venture out until the weather improved. Shortly before 9:00 AM, the power came back on. The TV weather comedians said the windy conditions might continue through Thursday. They were correct in that. After I removed the camera from the area of the feeder close to camp, I hiked down to the one in the hollow by the stream to switch SD cards and replace batteries. The photos from that camera showed three different bucks that had been hitting the corn there, one a nine-point that looked like he might be descended from Frank the Tank.

Thursday morning, the winds had let up considerably, and the weather was decent for a change. While I sat on the blowdown stand, I had quite a thrill when that same nine-point put in an appearance. Unfortunately, I never had a clear shot. This was a moose of a deer, easily weighing over 200 pounds. Had the stand been on the tree it was on last year, I probably would have had a clear shot, but so it goes. On the positive side, it was obvious that the bucks had entered what I call the "walking phase" of the rut where they spend most of the day traveling around looking for interesting does. I was not seeing many rubs yet, but the scrapes were very active.

That afternoon, I decided to try the hollow stand. While I did see deer, none came within range of my position. Five does made their way downhill just before the end of shooting light, too far away to shoot with the crossbow.

Friday turned out to be the best day of the week, weather wise. I did see one buck around 2:00 PM from the bear stand. As usual, I had no shot, but this one was not legal anyway, being only a four-point.

On Saturday morning, I hiked to the good stand and sat there until noon without seeing any deer. When it started to rain, I decided that I had enough of lousy weather for one week. I packed up and went home, listening to the Penn State game on the way. These guys do make it exciting. Another overtime win.

Larry and I opened camp for the final two weeks of archery deer season. That Wednesday, Dave joined us, and later in the week, Crawford appeared. After several days on stand, it became evident to us that the rut was beginning. The bucks definitely were in the walking phase. The guys who were hunting near the game lands food plots were seeing lots of sign in the form of numerous scrapes and rubs. On Friday morning, I sat on the brown ladder stand at the edge of the oak flat and had a spike walk past about thirty yards from me. Dave hunted from his pop-up blind early, and then later in the day walked down into Glade Hollow. After taking a short nap on top of a big rock there, he hunted outward from it and ran into a big buck that was chasing a doe. He thought the buck was that same nine-point I had the chance at the day before.

A nice ten-point visits the sand mound food plot

Larry took a shot at a five-point on Friday morning. He hit it in the neck and had a fair amount of blood for a short distance, but the blood trail ended. He searched for over an hour but found no more blood and did not recover the buck. Sunday morning, the four of us tromped through the laurel in an attempt to find the buck, but were not successful. Dave had to leave for home on Sunday. That left Larry, Crawford, and me to continue the hunt.

Since we had made a food plot out of the sand mound, I decided to put a game camera there. We did get some really good photos, including one of a ten-point.

On Monday, November 11, I sat on the laurel stand. Just as it started to get light enough to see, a small buck walked out from behind the hemlock tree in front of the stand. I took a twenty-yard shot, and he piled up a short distance from the stand. He was a five-point similar to the five-point Dave took a couple of years ago and will go into our record book as such. After taking the buck, two more bucks appeared in the same place. One of them freshened a scrape along the edge of the laurel while I watched. I field dressed the buck and then dragged him to the cabin, hanging him on our tripod to skin. Upon completing these tasks, I left for home at noon to take my deer carcass to the butcher. Crawford and Larry continued to hunt the rest of the day, intending to go home that evening before the impending snow.

Larry and I returned to camp on Wednesday to about two inches of fresh snow and cold temperatures. Dave rejoined us on Thursday. By then, warmer temperatures had caused most of the snow to melt. We hunted the rest of the week without seeing many deer. Had the full moon perhaps changed things? From checking the game cameras, we noticed that most of the activity was taking place at night. However, on Thursday morning at 7:15 AM while Dave and I made our way to our stands west of camp, our game camera took a photo of one eight-point buck feeding at the sand mound. A few of the bucks we got photos of were showing the results of rut battles in the form of broken tines and antlers.

Larry, in the process of recovering from leg surgery, tore his incision open while hiking much farther from camp than necessary. He had to quit hunting for the year, so he returned home on Saturday. Camp was not the same without him during bear and rifle deer seasons.

On Friday, November 22, Dave, Crawford, and I returned to camp to get ready for the opening of rifle bear season the next day. I made a huge pot of chili, using the burger from the bear I took last fall. It hit the spot, and the guys allowed as how I could make it again. When we checked the photos from the game cameras, we found that we still had four different bears in the area, so expectations were understandably high.

Saturday came in fairly mild, but the weather deteriorated toward afternoon with gusty winds and colder temperatures. By nightfall, a light lake effect snow was falling, and the temperatures dropped like a rock. Around noon, our neighbor Jim Procyson stopped in to visit. He had hiked the whole way from his home on Jersey Hollow Road which is well over a mile and two ridges from us. He was happily hoofing it all over the area in search of a bear.

Sunday, we did a few chores, set up Crawford's pop-up blind, filled the feeder in the hollow, and moved a couple of game cameras. While going up Harbaugh Road toward the game lands food plots, we crossed tracks of turkey, coyote, deer, and one huge bear. The bear's footprints could barely be covered by my boot sole. In my travel to the food plots to check on sign, I noted that none of the scrapes that had been so active a week ago were being freshened, so maybe the rut was over. Most of the rest of the day was spent watching pro football and eating, which is something that we also do very well.

Monday morning, the temperature on the porch was 11°. Since Crawford and Dave were leaving at noon, we decided to set up on stands until 9:00. Then Dave would put on a drive through the laurel on Craig's land. He found a lot of sign but was not successful in pushing a bear out to either of us. With a winter storm predicted for Tuesday, we decided that we had enough of bear hunting and left camp for home. Our game camera photos showed that the local bears were mostly nocturnal by this time.

Dave, Crawford, and I showed up in camp on Saturday, November 30, to get ready for the opener of rifle season. Since I had used my buck tag, I would be hunting on Mount Davis for does with my DMAP tag the first day. Crawford and Dave planned to hunt here at camp. I made a huge pot of ham and green beans which we worked on while watching football and getting our gear ready. Photos were downloaded from trail cameras. Since a few contained buck photos, we had high hopes as usual.

Several folks were expected in the Steinmiller camp, including Rick, his brother Ron, Chad, Craig and Steven Sabo, Uncle Al and his son-in-law Jimmy Yancy. Chad, Steven, and Jimmy visited us over the weekend. We suggested a couple of possible stands for Steven and Jimmy, which advice they took.

Monday morning, I left for Mount Davis an hour or so before first light. My plan was to hunt along the hollow that parallels Wolf Rock Road. I parked at the base of the gated logging road and hiked uphill for a quarter mile or so, taking a stand overlooking the hollow. I heard several gunshots as the day dawned. Two of them seemed really close. About 8:00, I saw movement to my left. Shortly, a six-point buck walked past me, presenting me with a perfect standing broadside shot at forty yards or so. That was all I saw until 11:00. I decided that since nothing seemed to be moving in the hollow, I would explore the hillside Dave liked to hunt across the road.

Upon hiking into the area, I found some huge boulders overlooking a laurel flat with a pond just beyond it. I climbed up on one of them and sat there on a milk crate some other hunter had left. After a short time, three does came past on their way to who knows where or for what reason. I touched off a round, and another batch of venison was mine. When I walked over to tag the doe, I discovered that I did not have a pen with which to fill out the tag, so I hiked back downhill to the truck to get one. I then dressed out the doe and made the drag of only a hundred yards or so back to the road and my truck.

Returning to camp, I hung the deer, skinned it out, and then hung the carcass in our shed to cool. Near dark, Crawford and Dave returned to camp. They had both seen a few does but no bucks. Both remarked that there had been very little shooting and none close to camp. Steven and Jimmy also had seen deer, but no shooters. This was the beginning of a very strange buck season. We were puzzled by the lack of buck kills anywhere close to camp. Crawford hunted most of the day on Tuesday and then returned home to hunt with some friends in Bedford County. Dave hunted the rest of the week out of camp and saw precious few deer. Nothing seemed to be moving. On Wednesday, I took my venison home, put it in the freezer, and returned to camp.

On Sunday, with a winter storm on the way, the three of us decided to call it a season and winterize the cabin. We drove home in a steady snowfall. It began to pile up by the time we left camp, but when I got home, there was only an inch or so on the ground in Saint Thomas.

In summary, we saw the smallest number of deer during the 2013 hunting season that we had ever seen, but the trail cameras do not lie. The deer were here. We also did not see any other hunters in the woods after the first couple of days. The best hunting happened during the peak of the rut when we all saw shooter bucks, and several of us had chances. We hoped that flintlock season after Christmas might be better. We did get some photos of bucks from the camera along the road close to the blowdown stand. A few of them survived to get us excited about next year. Hope springs eternal, and anyway, spring gobbler and trout seasons were coming soon!

Dave, Crawford, and Seth with two huge does taken in early muzzleloader season

2014: Mugs Arrives

As usual, the year began with Crawford, Dave, and me in camp for flintlock season. Flintlock season always opens the day after Christmas, but none of the gang could get to camp until after New Year's Day. Thursday, January 2, Dave and I arrived, and after getting a fire going, we hit the woods for the afternoon hunt. It began to snow, and this made for an interesting early evening hunt in what became a winter wonderland. At dark, after climbing down out of the stand and making my way toward camp, I jumped a single doe at our property line. That was the only deer seen by us.

Friday dawned windy and very cold. Dave decided to hunt out of his blind close to the game lands food plots. On the way, he would take down his trail camera near the blowdown stand. While trying to open the lock with nearly frozen fingers, five deer ran between him and the bear stand. Apparently, I moved them when I hiked into the woods. My walkabout down the hollow close to Glade Run ended up at Dave's blind, but I pushed no more deer past him. It was too cold to sit in a ladder stand, so I spent most of the day sneak hunting. Friday evening Crawford arrived, and we planned strategy for the next day.

Saturday morning, I hunted the laurel stand. Around 8:00, three deer passed just out of range. Dave and Crawford used the blowdown stand and one in Glade Run Hollow, but did not see any deer. The evening hunt was way more productive, at least in deer sightings. Crawford set up in the good stand where he saw two deer at sunset and then five more as darkness set in. He took two shots, but did not connect, so another flintlock hunt went into the books without any kills. That fact did not diminish our enjoyment of this very special time of the year.

Winter hit us with a vengeance in January. It got cold, stayed cold, snowed more than usual during January, and continued to do so in February. We never got out to camp during either month. One nice addition to the family occurred in January. Doris and I adopted Mugs, an English setter, from our local animal shelter. His former owner who lived alone, retired game warden Frank Clark, had died. We heard he may not have been discovered for a couple of days. His four dogs must have been traumatized by that.

Doris volunteers at the shelter and is on the board of directors. One Sunday, she found that two of the dogs were still there, a Gordon setter and a six-year-old English setter named Mugs. Knowing we had raised and campaigned English setters in the past and were familiar with the breed, she called me to ask if I was interested in seeing him. I came and took Mugs outside to a fenced area to see what he would do. Amazingly, he bonded with me almost immediately. From that point on, there was no question whose dog he was. Based upon what training he seemed to have, it appeared he would be a hunter. We didn't get to do much with him that winter because of the weather being what it was. I would later find out that his hunting instinct was way more than I had imagined.

I finally got an opportunity for a trip to camp the first week in March. Upon arriving, the driveway was open up to the parking area. The snow was over a foot deep with a lot of ice underneath. I got stuck and had to use a bag of Dave's sand to get out. After deciding not to spend the night, I took down the trail camera at the feeder and brought the SD card home. There were close to a thousand photos on it, mostly of does. At least three different bucks survived.

The next opportunity I had to visit camp was the first weekend in April, thinking that it might be time to turn on the water system and see how many leaks we had. Fortunately, this year there were none. It was a pleasure to once again be able to take a hot shower and use the flush toilet. When the water system is turned off, we have to use the job johnny in the shed. It has a very cold seat during winter. Nobody wants to be the first on really frigid mornings.

Friday, April 16, Mugs and I drove out to the cabin. I thought I might do some trout fishing on Saturday morning, but heavy rain got the creeks higher than I like, so I left the fishing to the diehards. Mugs and I went for a walk in the game lands fields. I thought there might be a pheasant or two left for him to find, but there were not. It didn't matter to Mugs. He enjoyed the run anyway.

Spring gobbler season finally arrived. Nobody else made the call. I was in camp alone the first weekend in May. That Saturday morning, I heard a single gobble very early and made my way toward the big rock, which seemed to be the area where the gobble originated. After calling for about half an hour, no more gobbles were heard. I worked my way out toward the area of the blowdown stand and sat on the rock next to the downed tree trunk that gave the blowdown stand its name. While there, six does and one of our local bears crossed Harbaugh Road behind me. No turkeys were either seen or heard.

Upon returning to camp, I noticed that the left front tire on my Ford Ranger was flat. Oh well. Time to learn about such things as where the jack and spare tire were located. I found the toy jack Ford includes in the package and had to read the manual to figure out how to get the spare disconnected from its mount. An hour later, I had the spare mounted. By then, all the tire shops anywhere would have been closed, so I decided to take a chance and drive home while the spare was looking good. I made it without further incident. On Monday morning, the nice folks at Service Tire in Chambersburg removed a nail and fixed the flat.

Wednesday, May 7, I returned to the cabin, hoping for another chance at a gobbler. That evening I went to several spots and called toward dusk, attempting to locate a gobbler for the next morning, but without any luck. Both Thursday and Friday mornings were among the quietest I had ever experienced at camp. Not a single gobble was heard from any direction. I did take a walk across the road past Scott's camp to see if anything was stirring in the bottom and saw several does making their way toward the swamp. Around 11:00 on Thursday morning, I decided to go trout fishing since the fish commission was scheduled to stock Laurel Hill Creek. Using a fly rod tipped with a wooly bugger, I managed to catch three trout. I kept one for dinner that evening. Grilled trout with hash browns makes a tasty meal.

Friday, after hunting the morning, I decided to return home. Doris and I love the spring book sale at Wilson College in Chambersburg that benefits Women in Need. I wanted to stock up on inexpensive reading material. The number of books at that sale, and the low prices for them, is amazing. Before leaving the area, I stopped at Rick Steinmiller's camp. Although it was close to 11:00 AM, only Uncle Al had gotten out of bed. Rick's sons, Chad and Hank, had joined him and Uncle Al for a weekend in camp. Al told me that he and Rick arrived first on Thursday evening. While they were getting settled in, Rick walked out the front door and almost ran into a resident bruin who was coming down the bank. I could still see the pug marks in the high grass where Al said the bear had walked. It was a close encounter of the black and furry kind. I have had several such encounters. One time while I sat on the cabin porch, a bear walked past the front steps. At such times, my heart pumps wildly. I am sure it was the same for Rick.

Memorial Day weekend, the Peters family journeyed to camp, hoping to spend a relaxing weekend. While Crawford toured the area on the ATV, tragedy struck in the form of a broken drive chain. The six-wheeler died at the bottom of the hill next to Drake Run. It sat there until Crawford and I made a trip to camp the following week to repair it. I also brought my Kubota tractor along to work on the drive, which subsequent rains washed out AGAIN. I suspected that the driveway was probably going to remain in rough shape as long as we owned the place. I took the tractor home that weekend and loaned it to Crawford so he could do some landscaping work at his house.

In mid-June, I took Crawford's trailer out to camp and brought the six-wheeler home for him to work on. He fixed the fuel leak. We hoped to get a few more years out of the old machine before having to replace it. ATVs are expensive.

Larry and I went to camp the last weekend of June. We spent a day staining the front porch. The next day, we hiked to the game lands food plots. Larry wanted to check a salt lick he had put out near the third food plot. It was not being used all that much. I found the camera Dave had put out near his pop-up blind and replaced the SD card. As we expected, not much was going on in that area. Once more, my Ford Ranger had a flat tire, this time on the right front. I got it changed and again, the folks at Service Tire did the flat fix. A new set of tires should be in order fairly soon.

The gang took a break in July and went north to Quebec for some walleye fishing on Lac Hebert. A great time was had by Dave, his son Matt, Larry, and me. Lots of walleye filets and potatoes fried in lard were consumed.

The second weekend in August, Larry and I made the trip to camp. Larry used his weed whacker to mow the growth on the sand mound while I cut a load of firewood. Larry got most of his mowing done until he was attacked by yellow jackets. They apparently did not like him disturbing their nest. This ended his mowing for the day. We eliminated the nest the next morning by using a wasp killer spray.

Toward the end of August, Doris, Mugs, and I drove out to camp. I finished cutting the poplar tree that I had downed earlier into logs and started splitting some of the smaller logs into firewood chunks. Mugs got to run around the area close to camp and enjoyed himself. He was still a hyperactive handful. Doris described him as "a seven-year-old puppy." We wondered whether he would ever grow up and slow down. My only worry was that he would encounter a rattlesnake or a bear.

The second week of September, Larry, Mugs, and I went to camp with the purpose of doing some bird hunting at On Point Outfitters. Their hunting area is close to the town of Addison, about ten miles from our camp. The afternoon hunt on Wednesday went pretty well in spite of 83° heat. Mugs found all six birds that were put out for us. We did not shoot all that well, getting only two of them. However, the purpose of the hunt was for Mugs to have some fun, and that was certainly accomplished. Thursday morning was windy and very humid. We found only two of the six birds put out and missed both. I guess we are not great shooters.

The following week we put up ladder stands on the game lands. The usual suspects (Dave, Larry, and I) were in camp. We set up the closer stands first. The next day, we hiked up the road toward the game lands food plots and carried stands in to their locations. We were now ready for archery deer season.

Archery season opened the first Saturday in October. Dave, Larry, and I showed up to hunt. We did not see many deer that first week. We never do. This is probably because most of the deer are hanging out closer to the corn and soybean fields half a mile distant. After the crops are harvested, things usually get much better in our part of the woods.

Because Dave had to work the following week, he went home Sunday. Larry and I hunted through Thursday of that second week. We sat on a number of the stands without seeing any deer, but that changed Thursday morning when both of us saw legal bucks. Early that morning while hunting the brown stand, a small buck with only one antler (three points) passed by and gave me a quartering away shot at ten yards, which I declined to take. It was too early in the season to settle for such a buck. Larry, hunting the stand at the rock, had a much bigger thrill. The buck that followed his trail into the area was a mature eight-point with heavy antlers. It never gave him a good opening for a shot though. At least it seemed that our luck might be changing. Unfortunately, rain was forecast for Friday. Having had enough of the lousy weather, we went home for the weekend.

I returned to camp alone the following Thursday afternoon and decided to hunt the blowdown stand that evening. About 6:15, three does made their way past the stand, milling around and feeding. They seemed to be working their way down the ridge parallel to the road. Two of them got onto the road and were eating acorns while the third one walked nearly under the stand. Strangely enough, I never had a clean shot at any of them. Finally, one of them having winded me, snorted, and the game ended with no score on my part.

Friday morning, I hunted the front stand and saw one deer. Because of the distance, I was not sure what it was. It might have been a buck since it was traveling alone. That afternoon, because it was raining, I hunted out of the box blind next to the sand mound. No deer were sighted.

Saturday, early muzzy season opened, so I decided to give the stand by the rock a try. The weather was fairly warm, but showers were predicted. The prediction was spot on. About 7:30, it started to rain, so I put up a tree umbrella temporarily. It made the hunting tolerable. About 8:15, a group of five does passed by at a considerable distance and went down into Alex Run. I never got a shot with the inline. While hunting in the condo to escape the rain that evening, I saw two does. Again, the distance and intervening brush prevented a decent shot. I came home early Sunday morning. By then, it was putting down a very wet snow. That week again produced some of the worst weather in which I have ever hunted three consecutive days at camp. Having had quite enough of it, I went home. (The reader should keep in mind that this is Somerset County, Pennsylvania. Weather wise, it is like being on another planet when compared to my home in Saint Thomas, just 90 miles to the east.)

On Wednesday evening, Larry and I showed up in camp for the "old folks" rifle doe season which would start the next day. Dave arrived Thursday around noon. That evening the first kill of the year was recorded when a large doe (about 140 lbs.) made a fatal mistake and walked into the good stand around 6:30 PM. One shot from the .257 Roberts ended her day. On a negative note, one of my game cameras had been removed and a business card from a WCO pinned on the tree. A contact with the WCO disclosed that I would be paying a fine to get my camera back. I had attached the camera to a tree using sheet metal screws, a violation that will not be repeated.

Most of Friday passed in uneventful fashion. Late that evening, Crawford and Seth arrived. Saturday was also the opening of pheasant season, and our experience shows that when the shotguns start popping, the deer move. Crawford and Seth chose the double stand in the hollow. Soon after they got there, two groups of does appeared. Seth picked out a big one and recorded his second one-shot kill. Later in the day, Dave also scored on a nice doe. We have to admit that the high-wheeled deer hauling cart he purchased makes dragging a deer out a whole lot less of a chore.

Monday, October 27, Larry and I took Mugs out for pheasants. While hunting on the game lands, we did find two cock birds. Although Mugs did his part, Larry and I did not. Sometime during the hunt, I injured my left knee. This prevented me from going back for the stocking later in the week, much to Mugs's displeasure. It remained to be seen how much this would impact my hunting in the future.

Near the end of the first week of November, I reinjured my left knee while walking out of the woods at dark. I hobbled the last two hundred yards back to camp using my crossbow as a crutch/walking stick. The doctor said I probably tore a ligament and did some cartilage damage. The soonest I could get an appointment was December 16.

The final week of archery deer season was very quiet as regards deer sightings, but ended well with Dave taking a real warrior of a buck on the morning of the last day. It had obviously been in some rutting battles and had lost most of one antler. Larry hunted the brown ladder one day and saw three rack bucks, but none were close enough to take a shot. I was relegated to stands within very easy hobbling distance of camp and did not see a single deer in four days of hunting, but one bear did amble by. The game camera at the sand mound indicated that we still had some bears in the area, including a sow with four cubs and a boar that was missing one eye. We named him "Old One Eye." Hopes were high for the upcoming bear wars. The week of archery bear season was in the "Record Cold" category. We left the cabin on Sunday, November 16, with a skiff of snow on the ground and flurries falling. The temperature at camp dropped from there on throughout the week, leaving me wondering what I might find when I got back on Thursday. Frozen pipes are always a possibility, and that can cause major damage. I need not have worried. The pipes were fine, and the water system had no damage whatsoever.

Dave's 2014 buck

Dave, his nephew Judd, Crawford, and I were present for bear season, but no bears made any sort of appearance during the daytime. Night was a different story. The game camera again captured the sow with four cubs and one boar bear. Where they went during the daytime was a mystery we would have to solve. Judd saw fifteen deer while hunting at the bear stand. Ronnie Steinmiller showed up on Sunday to visit. Other than us, he was the only person in camp along Back Road.

The first week of rifle deer season was a washout. Literally! It poured rain the first day, and the weather went downhill from there with rain five out of the six days. During the week, we saw a grand total of two other hunters in the woods. No deer were taken, and we left for home on Saturday after winterizing the cabin.

In summary, this may not have been a super year when it came to harvesting game, and the weather did give us fits. I worried about the injuries to my knees. Both of them were in bad shape. This would seriously limit my hunting unless they got better.

2015: *One For The Books*

January, 2015, began for me with a pair of gimpy knees left over from injuring both of them during the past hunting season. This would seriously detract from the enjoyment of hunting. I did not hold out much hope for success since I was very limited in how well I could walk to hunting spots. Oh well. We do the best we can, and, boy-oh-boy, was I going to be surprised at how this year turned out!

Crawford, Dave, and I journeyed to camp the first weekend of the new year. As was usual, this opened the primitive weapons season for us. While we did see deer, nobody scored. A light skiff of snow on the ground, with no bear tracks showing anywhere, indicated that bears were not out of their dens, but deer had returned to the area near our camp. Lots of tracks led to our feeder.

That last weekend of flintlock season turned out to be the coldest so far with a stiff northwest wind. Dave decided to go to camp alone and arrived to find the cabin inside temperature in the mid-thirties. It took nearly a day to get the cabin warm, and Dave stated that the first night was a cold one for sleeping. He hunted the mini-condo next to the sand mound that evening. When he returned to the cabin, a half dozen deer, including one buck, were at the feeder. He saw more deer that weekend than we were used to seeing during the fall seasons, but he got no shots off and took no game. Dave began the process of taking down stands by bringing the rock and the Glade Run stands in on his deer cart.

The following weekend, all four of us regulars made it to camp for our annual workday during which we finished removing and storing ladder stands. We now had thirteen ladder stands which gave us a lot of flexibility in hunting the area around camp. As the weather was supposed to get worse on Sunday, we left camp early in the morning, planning to beat the snowstorm. Before leaving, we filled the feeder and set up cameras so we could get photos of the animals coming in. I hoped to return sometime in the next week since I did have a bobcat tag to fill, if possible.

On the way home, Dave and I stopped at Rick Steinmiller's camp. Ronnie's son Mike and a buddy were there for the weekend. They had no water since the water system had not been drained and the filter bowls had frozen and burst. We returned to our camp and retrieved the filter system that we had disconnected when we installed the iron filter, hoping that they could use it. We don't know whether or not they were successful with repairs.

During the winter season, I made a number of trips out to camp. Unfortunately, I again had no success in filling that bobcat tag. My knees had improved a little, but it was still painful to walk. This limited how far I could travel to do winter inventory. Dave injured his wrist at work, causing him some discomfort and limiting his ability to ply his trade as a mason. Snow accumulated as usual. By early March there may have been a foot and a half on the ground near the cabin. Finally, it started to warm up.

On Wednesday, March 11, the temperature on the porch was close to 60°, and what snow remained was melting and slushy. Deer tracks and scat were everywhere in the area of camp. We did a walkabout with Dave's route being along the edge of Glade Hollow from Craig's wooden stand out toward the big rock and back along the cabin side of the ridge. He found four shed antlers, three of them under one hemlock tree. I decided to tour the northern slope along Drake Run where the snow was still over a foot deep. I found no sheds, but noted that the deer were bedding under hemlocks where the snow was nowhere near as deep. That evening we watched ten deer come in to the feeder. One was a huge doe with her twin fawns from the previous year. The last three to come in were bucks with antler buds just starting to become visible.

Larry's back was giving him problems, and Dave was working to support his fishing habit, so most of the times during April and May I was by myself. The feeder got visited on a regular basis by both deer and turkeys. On one occasion, a group of ten squirrels could be seen eating the corn. One of them was rusty red in color. It may have been a fox squirrel. Another time, while some hens fed on the corn, two big gobblers put on a show for me, strutting and gobbling in the driveway right in front of the cabin. Seeing the critters at the feeder always adds a huge amount of enjoyment to being in camp.

On April Fool's Day, I journeyed out to Pittsburgh and met Jim Kull who was buying one of my rifles. Jim had brought along his wife Candy and his dog. I believe anyone who has a dog and takes it along for rides is a good person. After that, I continued on to camp to spend some quality time. I fired up the chainsaw, but a sudden backache ended the firewood cutting. The foamers were cold, and the critters coming in to the feeder kept me amused. The next morning, I got up to the sound of two gobblers making their springtime music from the slope on Craig's property. Since my back was feeling somewhat better, I started sawing up the downed red oak on Craig's property. He gave me permission to use it for firewood, and I hauled a load of logs to split at a later time. Photos downloaded from the camera at the feeder showed that a sow with cubs was coming in, and some of the bucks had started to grow this year's antlers.

On Friday, May 1, I went to camp for the spring gobbler opener. Again, I was alone. Crawford had a retirement party to attend, Dave was tournament salmon fishing, and Larry was working on some health issues. Nobody was hunting out of any of the other camps either. This amazed me since we had been hearing and seeing a few gobblers.

Saturday morning, I made my way into the woods at full moon. No flashlight was necessary. At least four different gobblers were sounding off as daylight approached, one of which was down in Drake Run hollow near the good stand. I decided to set up on the hillside above it near the blowdown stand. Good choice, but not so good results. Two gobblers and four hens fed past me at a distance of close to eighty yards. No matter how skillful I thought my calling was, neither gobbler would detour away from his harem. I didn't hear a single gunshot all morning, which surprised me.

I spent Saturday afternoon working the chainsaw and piling up some wood to split. Sunday afternoon I split a load to take home later. Sunday evening while sitting on the porch close to dark, I heard one gobbler sound off. It seemed he was in the area of the laurel stand, so I thought I might set up along the old woods road that goes from the blowdown to the rock.

Monday morning turned out to be one of those mornings that you live for. It was on the cool side at just over 40°. Not a breath of a breeze stirred the leaves on the trees, and as the sky brightened, not a cloud could be seen. I heard several gobbles. One in particular seemed to be coming from the area of the blowdown stand. I sat with my back to a beech tree, waiting for things to develop, and develop they did!

When I started to hear turkeys stirring in the treetops, I did a few tree yelps and clucks. Shortly after that, I did a coming down off the roost cackle and some feeding putts. Immediately a gobbler sounded off. The sound usually makes the hairs on the back of my neck bristle. This time was no exception. I took a few deep breaths to steady my nerves, and then I did a few yelps and some more feeding clucks. My reward came in the form of a lusty gobble, followed by a black object appearing on the old logging road to my left. As the scene continued to develop, it turned out to be two big gobblers. Wow! I had a choice! The bigger one was doing the gobbling, so I focused on it. As his head went behind a tree, I adjusted my position. When it emerged, I squeezed the trigger, and my spring gobbler season ended. My prize was a twenty-pound bird with a beard just less than ten inches long and one inch spurs. Nobody else being in camp, this hero shot was the best I could do.

2015 turkey gobbler and an old guy with bad knees

Since turkey hunting had come to an end for me, I spent most of the rest of the month doing chores around camp. These included getting the cabin walls cleaned and ready for staining and cutting firewood. Several bears put in an appearance. On one occasion, a sow with four cubs fed on the corn. Two other single bears, one a huge boar, also showed up to feed. Another time, a bear walked up the path from the feeder to the cabin, making me consider how safe I was on the porch.

The time had come to put a coating of stain on the exterior cabin walls. Dave, Larry, and I participated. Since we had scaffolding, Dave suggested that we put it up to do the job, and it did make the project much easier and safer. The stain we used this time was Carbolineum, an oil based, penetrating stain. It should be far superior to the CWF stain we applied the first time we did this.

Dave climbs the scaffolding during the staining project.

Some of us went to camp several times during the summer. Larry decided to plant a turnip patch on top of the sand mound. By summer's end, it was growing nicely. Deer like turnips. They usually graze on the tops during summer and fall. In the wintertime, they will actually dig up the roots and snack on them.

The second weekend in September saw Dave and me in camp for the weekend. We spent Friday hauling a stand up to the oak flat above the game lands food plots. The game commission folks mowed both plots completely for a change instead of just taking a trip around the edges. We did not find much in the way of acorns, but it was a bit early yet. Some white oak acorns were found on the driveway into camp. This raised hopes that we could have a good white oak year. White oak acorns are preferred by deer, turkeys, and bears. When they are abundant, so are the animals.

We checked to see if the stands we left in the hollow and the laurel stand were still there. Later, we removed the ladder stand Rick Steinmiller called the metal stand. Rick asked us if we would do this because the new owners of the land Rick Sabo sold did not appear to be neighborly and wanted it taken down.

Saturday, the rains came. Dave and I drove to Somerset and did some shopping at Lowes. We purchased lumber and hardware needed for enclosing the stairway to the upstairs and putting in a door. Gravity being what it is, a lot of the heat goes upstairs when the woodstove is operating. This should make sleeping in the bunkroom on the second floor more comfortable. I put the finishing touches on the carpentry the second week of September.

During this time, several nice bucks were coming in to the feeder. One looked like an eight-point, and the second might have been a seven. On Sunday, while driving past the Waley farm, a flock of turkeys crossed the road in front of me.

Dave and I ventured out to camp the third week in September. I got there after a short stop at Highland's Tire Shop near Bedford to find out why a tire inflation warning was showing on the dash of my Ford Ranger. The guys there determined that I had a bad sensor that would be expensive to replace. I "fixed" it by placing a piece of black tape over the warning light so I can't see it. I will check tire pressure the way I always have, with a tire gauge.

I arrived at camp around noon to find Dave waiting at the gate. We ate some lunch and then got busy taking stands out into the woods. Over the next three days, we put up all of the stands that we had taken down last winter. We moved Dave's stand from along the road in the hollow below camp to a tree below the sand mound. We also rotated the stand on the other side of the hill close to Craig's front wooden stand. It now faced in the direction Larry wanted it to. We were ready to hunt deer.

On Thursday, we had a visit from Glenn Durbin and his son, also named Glenn. At the time they arrived, Dave was trimming brush along the driveway. Mr. Durbin bought a rifle from me, and we visited for an hour or so. They showed us photos of some of the deer they have taken on their Eastern Shore property in Maryland. Wow! After some discussion of how handy it is to have Dave around camp, Glenn suggested that I write a story entitled, "Every Camp Needs A Dave." (I will included that story in another book I am writing, THE LUCKIEST HUNTER WITH ONE FOOT IN THE GRAVE.)

Saturday, I split up a rank of wood while Dave did a walkabout. He drove over to Scott Camp Road and parked at the game lands gate with the aim of walking out that road to find the chestnut tree grove we had been told was there. He found it about half a mile from the gate, almost directly across Glade Run from the rock stand. About thirty trees are growing there, and the year's crop of chestnuts littered the ground. He saw a flock of turkeys and a lot of deer and bear sign, with many buck rubs in that area. Later, when he crossed Glade Run and climbed to the oak flat where the brown stand is located, he also found plenty of deer sign there. This was great news.

Archery deer season opened the first weekend of October. Larry and I made the trip out to camp on Friday, October 2, in a pouring rain. The rain continued for a good portion of the day on Saturday. We did not make the call for the morning hunt. Both of us were getting too old to sit out in the rain. The skies cleared somewhat that afternoon, so Larry went to the front stand, and I chose the laurel stand. About 5:00, I was treated to the sight of a bear working its way through the laurel toward me. Amazing as it might be, the bear was a rusty red color phase, sometimes called cinnamon, which is quite rare in Pennsylvania. I snapped a photo of it with my cell phone, but this phone does not take very high-quality photos. We never saw this bear again, but we found out that someone did get it during the rifle bear season. Larry also saw a bear, this one being black. Later toward dark, three deer passed the laurel stand, but at too great a distance to shoot.

On Monday, Larry toughed it out on the rock stand for most of the day. I sat in the new stand below the sand mound in the morning. When returning to camp, I saw two does crossing the food plot next to the feeder. For the evening hunt, I chose the blowdown stand. Neither of us saw any deer. As Larry's back was giving him some pain, he decided to go home Tuesday morning. I did also. We planned to try again during the early muzzy season. I had another hunting trip booked for Deerfield Plantation in South Carolina the second week of October.

The Deerfield hunt turned out to be one with mixed success. Most of the week, the days were way too warm for good hunting, and we saw very few deer. A week earlier, a flood had closed much of their best hunting area, which they call the brown and down tract. This section has no antler restrictions, so any deer is legal game there. We got to hunt that section only one time, the last evening of our hunt. Our group took eight deer, four of them being bucks. I got lucky and managed to take a nice eight-point and a spike.

The week of early muzzy season began on Tuesday for us when Dave and I drove to camp. During this season, only does are legal game if one hunts with a muzzle loading firearm. Both bucks and does are legal when hunting with archery tackle. We started hunting that evening, but spotted no deer. Thursday and Friday, we journeyed to Mount Davis and did see deer, but none were close enough for shooting. Larry and Crawford arrived on Friday. Hopes were high on Saturday since the bird hunters usually move deer to us, but the only deer seen by any of us that morning were two bucks on the front stand. One of them, an eight-point, gave me a standing broadside shot at ten yards, but I had the wrong weapon with me.

Crawford and I tried to fix the leak in the back porch bunkroom roof on Sunday by putting a piece of rubber on top of the shingles. (This did not work. We would later have to solve the problem by installing a metal roof.)

Back home on the following Monday and Tuesday, I took Mugs bird hunting at Royal United, an outfit near Fort McCord about seven miles from Saint Thomas. Mugs did a great job. He found all of the birds planted for us, but the shooter was not so great. If I managed to shoot one, he retrieved it. He is one of the best setters I have ever had, and I thoroughly enjoy hunting with him.

Dave's 2015 buck

Dave continued his hunt the last week of October, and I joined him on Thursday. The weather had cooled then, and the rut kicked in. On Friday morning, Dave got two shots at bucks from the bear stand. The first shot was a clean miss (He found the arrow.) at a really nice buck, probably an eight-point. His second shot was true, and after some tracking, he called me to bring the cart. I helped him load the buck on the cart and cleared some pathways for him. At the time, I thought this was a pretty big deer. When we got it back to camp, we put the chest tape on it. Dressed weight by the tape was just over the 149 pound line, so we recorded it as a 150 pound buck. As is the case with nearly all of our deer, this one was rolling fat. Tooth succession disclosed its age as two and a half years. This buck had a strange rack. It had a long spike with a funny growth where the brow tine would have been on the right side and four points on the left side.

We returned to the cabin the following Thursday. Dave and Larry got there first. I made a stop in the town of Springs, Pennsylvania, to pick up my new Horton Storm crossbow at Arrowhead Outdoors. The owner, Mike Wisman, had set up the bow perfectly. The first few shots I took were dead center bullseyes, so I thought I might be ready to end the season's drought, buck wise.

While Dave would have a couple of close encounters with a ten-point at his ground blind, Larry and I had to be satisfied with seeing a few does. No shots were taken until Monday, November 9, when I scored on a huge nine-point. This happened early in the morning while I hunted out of the mini condo overlooking the turnip patch on the sand mound. A doe emerged from the woods along the camp driveway and fed on the turnip tops. A buck followed. My breathing quickened, as I could tell he was big one. He was busy chasing a doe and had no idea anything could possibly go wrong. Something did, at least for him. The crossbow bolt hit him exactly where I was aiming, and we found the bolt the next day. It passed completely through both lungs. The buck ran downhill on the other side of the sand mound and piled up next to a hemlock tree below it. He was way too heavy for a cripple like me to drag back to camp, so I got the six-wheeler and a rope to do the dragging. The PGC's chest tape disclosed his weight to be 217 pounds live and 184 pounds dressed. This was the heaviest buck I had ever taken in Pennsylvania. He was only a little heavier than my 2009 buck, a six-point (which weighed ten pounds less), but this one had a much nicer rack.

Dave and Larry continued to hunt most of this last week of archery deer season, but toward the end of the week, Larry's back acted up once again, so he went home on Friday morning. I also left for home, having a honeydo chore scheduled for Saturday.

Friday evening, Dave called to antagonize both Larry and myself with a report that while hunting from the mini condo overlooking the sand mound, he sighted five bucks in that one evening. Two spikes, a four-point, our raghorn with four on one side, and a nice eight-point all came to check the area in their search for a hot doe. Dave stated that, had Larry stuck it out, he would have had no problem filling his buck tag with the raghorn. The eight-point may have presented more difficulty.

The author with a nice Pennsylvania whitetail

Friday, November 20, the gang assembled for rifle bear season. I jumped the gun by hunting two days for bear with the crossbow, but did not see any bears nor any sign of them. We did not even have any photos of bears on the game cameras, so I wasn't holding out much hope for bear season. Dave and Judd rolled in that afternoon, followed by Crawford and his buddy John, also known as "Deadeye." We partied a bit that evening, but made the call bright and early on Saturday morning. All journeyed to their chosen stands.

Right away in the morning, the Giovannitti camp and their hunters put on a drive in Glade Run Hollow, but were not successful in moving any bears. Most of the shooting we heard, and we did hear more than most previous years, seemed to be coming from the area around Ursina, with some near Cranberry Lake. There was absolutely nothing heard close to camp.

That afternoon, Dave and I went to the Giovannitti camp and left a note asking whether or not we could get together for some drives on Monday. Mark got back to me that evening and suggested we visit on Sunday, which we did. Crawford and John left on Sunday to return home. Dave, Judd, and I stayed to work on filling a bear tag. In our visit to the Giovannittis, we made plans for them to meet at our camp on Monday at 6:30 AM. We did three drives that morning in the area of camp, but moved only deer and turkeys. One buck sighted on the first drive was a huge ten-point that walked almost under the hollow double stand. After the third unsuccessful drive, John McDermott, who hunts with the Giovannitti group, suggested that we try one last push over on the western edge of Somerset County along Augustine Road. The area driven was in Lower Turkeyfoot Township, Somerset County, only a few hundred yards from the Fayette County line.

The drivers walked over half a mile east on Augustine Road and then dropped downhill toward the Youghiogheny River to form their skirmish line. As with many drives, the two on the bottom of the line went slightly off course, farther downhill than intended, which was fortunate since they probably were the ones who drove a bear uphill. We speculated that when the bear got in sight of Augustine Road, someone may have been walking there or a vehicle was going by, so he altered course to the east. This brought him past my stand position. I found an opening in his path, and when his head hit my sight, I squeezed the trigger. The bear dropped on the spot. I had made a slightly lucky shot and hit him in the neck, breaking it cleanly. I then yelled out, "Bear down!" There was some confusion below me, and someone yelled, "Where?" A couple of the other guys were standing there talking when I touched off the shot thinking the drive was over. I don't think they believed me when I yelled, but when the group arrived on the spot, we were in possession of a genuine black bear.

The bear gang with the finale of my triple trophy year

2015: One For The Books | 159

I'm not sure who was the happiest among the hunters. Mark later told me that this was the first bear the group had taken, really a great thing for them. Lots of back slapping and photo-taking ensued. Then four of the younger guys each grabbed a paw, and up the hill they went with the bear.

Back at camp, we loaded the bear on Dave's pickup and made the trip to the game commission's bear check station in New Centerville with our prize. After doing so, we returned to camp and skinned it, putting the carcass into the shed to cool. We butchered it the next day. Around this time, it entered my thinking for the first time that I had taken all three big game animals in a single year. At one time, the game commission gave a triple trophy award for such an achievement. They discontinued it during the 1970s. This did not matter very much to me. Having done it was its own reward.

Rifle deer season began November 30 this year. The day before, Larry, Dave, and I hit the camp. Dave and I, having filled our buck tags, intended to hunt the Mount Davis DMAP area. Larry still had a buck tag to fill, so he would hunt at camp. The day was wet and cold with a light drizzle. Dave and I returned to camp midafternoon having had enough of that weather. Larry decided to spend the evening portion of the day in the mini condo next to the sand mound. Wouldn't you know it, the raghorn put in an appearance, and Larry scored. This made us three for three on bucks with a bear and a turkey gobbler thrown in. It was by far, the most successful season we had since we moved to Camp Rip-N-Tear.

While Crawford chose to hunt back home in Fulton County, both he and Seth ended up being successful. Seth took a smaller buck that Crawford finished off for him. Crawford, while hunting in Letterkenny, took a really big eight-point. I remembered thinking back in January that with such bad knees, this would not be much of a year. For me, it certainly turned out to be one for the books.

2016: The Year From Hell

January rolled around as it usually does, but with considerably less snow. I was nursing two really bad knees, so I skipped the primitive weapons season. The other guys did manage to get in a few days of flintlock hunting and took down the stands that were on game lands. Some deer, including a few nice bucks, did survive the 2015 hunting season.

After reading the following few paragraphs, the reader will understand why I refered to this particular year as "the year from hell." On January 5, I entered our Chambersburg hospital to get both knees replaced. Dr. Roger Robertson, a local orthopedic surgeon, did the job. I spent considerable time recuperating and doing physical therapy/rehab. Another setback happened on February 7 when Ms. Doris had a stroke and was hospitalized for a couple of days. Within a few weeks she nearly completely recovered but wondered why she had the stroke in the first place. She has always been in top physical condition and healthy, but these things happen. Dave and Larry made several trips out to camp to fill the feeder and download photos of the game visiting it. During these two months, Dave stopped by the house to make sure Doris and I had wood and coal sufficient to keep warm. By the beginning of March, things had improved somewhat, and we had resumed walking up to a mile and a half.

During the second week of March, I began to experience extreme fatigue. All I wanted to do was to sit around and rest, basically doing nothing at all, which some might find to be enjoyable. I did not. By the end of the week it had become problematic. To top it off, I had developed a hacking cough. (I won't describe the oysters so as not to offend the sensitive.) The following Monday night I had a coughing spell that lasted over half an hour, and I think the only reason it stopped was because I got so tired, I couldn't cough anymore. Five minutes later I broke out in full body hives, which is no pleasure as those who have had this can testify.

The next day, things went downhill in a big way. Twice, while just walking from one room in the house to another, I passed out and fell down. There were no major injuries to anything but my pride, and perhaps a bruise deep in my gluteus maximus. Ms. Doris, in her infinite wisdom, had enough, and we pursued medical remedy by going in to the local emergency ward, fully expecting to hear the word, pneumonia.

Upon entering the triage part of the ward, one of the first things they did was to weigh me and do an EKG. My weight had fallen from my normal robust 185-190 pounds to 162 since the knee replacement on January 5. The EKG proved to be the kicker, however, as it disclosed something abnormal. It was a shock when the doctor asked, "How long have you had a-fib?" This is a condition (atrial fibrillation) where the upper chambers of the heart are not pumping as strongly as usual and blood tends to pool in the right atrium with the potential to form very thick blood which can later cause clots to form. These could lead to a stroke or heart attack.

A flurry of activity on the part of the ER staff occurred, and within several hours I found myself having been admitted to the cardiac care unit where they got my heart rate stabilized. The pneumonia was shoved to second place. (It don't rain 'lest it pours.) Benadryl brought the hives under control, at least for most of the time. I also acquired a cardiologist, Dr. Adenike, who over the next few months would subject me to a battery of tests to determine just how bad things were. As it turned out, they were not all that bad. I had several visits from friends while in the hospital, notably Crawford Sr., Dave, and Larry. After two days in the hospital, I returned home with several new prescriptions in hand (better living through chemistry, or some such) and feeling somewhat improved. Ms. Doris hovered over me like a momma bird and had worked out a system where I took those pills at certain times of the day. In the words of my cousin Lynn, who is a few years older than I am, "Gettin old ain't for sissies." I am a tough old bird and would be in the woods soon. After all, there were turkeys to scout and trout waiting to be caught.

Another tragedy occurred during this trying time. Roo, our Australian cattle dog, passed away at the age of sixteen. She had been adopted from the local animal shelter ten years before and was much loved. Her health had gone downhill recently. This reminded me that our furry friends do not live as long as we do.

Tuesday, April 5, Dave, Larry, and I ventured out to camp. We filled the feeder and did a few walkabouts. One of four sheds Dave found on the hike was a nice five-point antler near the laurel stand. With the weather being on the warm side, we enjoyed the porch that evening and returned home the next day.

Dave with a foamer and the results of a morning shed hunt

Because the weather comedian predicted snow and very cold temperatures on Saturday, April 9, I decided to return to camp on Friday, April 8, and fire up the wood stove so that the pipes would not freeze. This ended up being a good idea, because the temperature on Sunday bottomed out at 15°. My visit to camp had been interesting in that we had lots of traffic at the feeder, including three big long beards Friday afternoon. They returned during the snowstorm on Saturday. I tried to snap a photo of them from the front porch, but was not successful. When the outside temp hit 25° Monday morning, I stoked the wood stove and departed for home. The forecast said this should be the last sub-freezing temperature for awhile.

April 30, the opening day of spring gobbler season, wasn't too bad a day in Somerset County. It was partly cloudy, but really dark when I got up at 5:00. As usual, I brewed a pot of coffee and took the first cup out to the front porch while listening for gobbles. At 5:45, or thereabouts, I heard the first one. It sounded like it was coming from the hollow below camp and out to the west, so I got my stuff together and made a quarter mile hike to the blowdown stand. I let the woods settle a bit and then did a few tree yelps. No response. As the sky brightened, I decided to do the coming down cackle followed by some feeding clucks. One halfhearted gobble sounded in response from the hollow below me. Hey, this was progress, right? I settled in for the long haul, my back against a big white oak, facing downhill and on the eastern side of the saddle (a dip in the ridge crest).

About 6:30, I saw a turkey. It was a hen, and she was heading uphill toward the other side of the saddle. If she continued in the direction she was going, she would pass me at a distance of eighty yards. This would have been an easy rifle shot, but not in range for the scattergun. A second hen appeared, and then the gobbler showed. He strutted four or five times while following the hens, but apparently they were playing hard to get. I tried everything, including aggressive hen calls, but no way would they change course. I guess two birds in the hand would be worth way more to a gobbler than one you can't see in the bushes. Later in the morning, I was surprised by a jake who came in to my hen calls. I could have shot him, but after seeing the gobbler this morning, I decided to hold out a little longer.

Thinking that I should give it another try, I drove out to camp on Sunday, May 8. The weather comedian had been predicting nice weather for Monday and Tuesday. Monday turned out to be a fairly nice morning, but by 10:00, a light rain had begun. Off and on rain continued most of Monday and into Tuesday. Not a gobble was heard in the mornings. Would this spring gobbler season go into the books as a complete failure? Possibly so. Several other times when I had a chance to go out and hunt for the gobblers, it rained, so I finally gave up. Maybe next year would be better.

During June, I drove out to camp a couple of times. I wanted to mow the lawn around the cabin, but first I had to get the old John Deere mower started. I took the carburetor apart and cleaned out the orifice, then used fresh gasoline and a squirt of starting ether. It took right off, so I finally mowed the lawn. Emboldened by my experience with the mower, I decided to tackle my old Poulan string trimmer. I repeated the procedure above, then put new gas in the tank. After a squirt of starting fluid, the darned thing ran for the first time in three years. I took it to the sand mound to cut the grass and weeds there.

The following week, Dave and I went to camp, hoping to get some work done on a couple of food plots. Dave loaded my Troy rototiller in his truck and left for camp around 8:00. I left later and arrived there around noon. Dave had already finished weed whacking the sides of the sand mound and was working on the top, intending to plant turnips there once again. After he finished rototilling the sand mound, I tilled five strips in the food plot next to camp and planted ladino clover in them. Following lunch, Dave took the rototiller to the food plot in the hollow next to the stream. He reported that the soil there was superb. He planted brassica in that plot. Meanwhile, I fired up the chainsaw and cut some firewood which I hauled to camp in the six-wheeler.

The next morning, I split the wood I had cut previously and stacked it on the porch. Dave and I then added one of the four ranks of wood from our woodpile to it. We were just about ready for next winter. Larry had planned to come along, but then said he had other things he needed to do. Dave and I left for home later in the day. I dropped the feeder bin off at Crawford's house for him to repair. The spreader mechanism rusted loose and was found on the ground where it landed.

During the summer, we visited camp frequently to cut more firewood and just hang out. Hanging out is one of the wonderful things about having a hunting camp. I was by myself on Saturday, August 13. While putting food in the refrigerator, I looked to the left of it and saw a blacksnake skin about five feet long. A big one for sure. I searched the cabin but did not find him, so I have to assume he ate some of our resident mice and passed on to the next hunting ground.

One day in August, I downloaded photos from the game cameras. The best of the pictures showed three nice bucks at the salt lick. The buck on the left with only the top of his head visible had a non-typical rack with six points on one side and four on the other. The middle buck, smallest of the three, appeared to be a ten-point. The one on the right was a huge eight-point. A really mature buck will have a belly, and this one did. All three were in velvet. Our game cameras have taken some photographs of big bucks, but this one might be the best of all. We have never had three such bucks in one photo.

Three exceptional bucks in velvet visit the salt lick.

The last weekend in August I invited a group I know from a message board, the PFSC board, to camp for a "bull shooting" session. I arrived on Friday and did some prep work for the cooking of chili plus ham and green beans. Dave and Larry showed up later, and we sat on the porch enjoying the evening.

On Saturday morning, we had a decent sized bear come in and stuff himself at the feeder while we sipped our morning coffee. After breakfast, Dave and Larry did a bit of tilling and planting in our food plots while the pots of chili and ham and green beans simmered. The plot next to the creek was being hit hard by deer. Around 10:30, the first two of the bull shooters, Dutch and Gal That Fishes, arrived together. They were followed closely by Turkeykiller. Around noon, GlennD drove in. He brought a case of Belgian Fat Tire beer, so we started to sample that and the bear chili, which experts allowed was pretty decent. The Gal contributed a few dishes, one of which was a concoction made from a chicken of the woods mushroom. DaveT arrived mid-afternoon, bringing with him two of his finely restored rifles for us to see, and also a case of Stella Artois.

Most of the participants in the bull shooting session. From left: Larry, Dave, Tom (Turkeykiller), Brad (Dutch), Kathy (Gal That Fishes), GlennD, and the author. DaveT took the photo.

Toward evening, after lots of stories were told and a fair amount of beer had been consumed, the party broke up. Dave, Larry, and I stayed in camp.

On Sunday morning while making a phone call home, I was told that Doris needed to have our cat Trouble put down after a huge blood clot developed that cut off all circulation to his hind quarters during the night. This was diagnosed as something called saddle thrombosis. Trouble was about ten years old. He showed up one day, looking for a place to stay, and we gave him one. He had become a nice cat in later years and was part of the family. We will miss him.

During August, I bruised my left index finger on the latch to our boat cabin at Lake Raystown. I didn't think it would be anything serious, but it did not heal. One day in mid-September, Ms. Doris convinced me to stop at Med Express in Chambersburg and get it checked out. A nice doctor examined it and ordered X-rays. Lo and behold, a portion of the end bone in that finger had disappeared. No, I am not joking. She told me to make an appointment with my orthopedic practice and get them involved. She also faxed the X-rays to Carey Strong, my CRNP. What else could go wrong this year? The diagnosis was that I had a bone infection which destroyed some of the last part of my finger bone. Recommendation: amputate at the distal joint. This was scheduled for November 2. Fortunately, my left index finger is not my trigger finger. Unfortunately, this would put a huge crimp on my hunting during the rut.

Our moose hunting trip to Newfoundland, scheduled the previous year, happened the end of September, with us returning October 4. Dave, Larry, Steve Musser, and I had a great time, even though the only moose brought home was Dave's. We missed the opening of archery deer season, but tried to make up for it by hunting hard from then on.

The weekend of October 8 found Crawford, Dave, and myself in camp, enjoying a hard rain Friday evening into Saturday. In spite of the rain, we did carry in and set up five ladder stands. The only one remaining to be put in was the blowdown stand. The game cameras took lots of photos of deer and bears. One very positive thing was that the white oak acorn crop looked good this year.

I returned to camp for the early muzzleloader season on Thursday, October 13. On Friday morning, while hunting in the mini condo, a group of does came out to feed on the sand mound turnip patch, and I took one for the freezer. The next day, while sitting in the same stand, two bucks came past me. I watched a six-point freshen a scrape on the edge of the driveway, and then a big boy showed up to freshen it as well. I passed up a shot at the six-point and thought I might regret that later. Both bucks were still hanging around, so I hoped I might have another chance at one of them. That afternoon, I hunted out of the laurel stand and saw two does, but did not shoot.

As it would be my last chance to hunt before scheduled surgery on my left index finger, I went to camp Tuesday evening, October 25, and planned to stay until the following Monday. Thursday, it rained most of the day. I don't hunt in the rain anymore. On Friday, I hunted from the bear stand. The only deer I saw was the ten-point with six points on his right side. It passed by without giving me any sort of shot. Bummer. As it turned out, this was the only one of those three bucks in the previous photo that anyone had a chance at while hunting that year.

Saturday, I went down to the big condo. Three bucks walked by. All of them were small ones, so I did not shoot. While sitting there and contemplating things, I got a wild idea. Why not put up a stand across the road from the scrape close to the mini condo (mentioned above)? The more I thought about it, the better I liked the idea, so I did it that afternoon. Dave showed up on Sunday, and we discussed the placement of the new stand along the driveway. He agreed that I should hunt the next morning, as Monday, October 31 (which was Halloween), would be my last day to hunt before finger surgery. I hoped to make it a good one.

Monday morning turned out to be cool, about 40°. What breeze there was came from the north, perfect for that new stand. At 7:45, I saw a couple of does feeding on the sand mound. A half-hour later, a buck appeared in the woods and prepared to cross the driveway to my left. I had a good broadside shot as he stopped at the edge. My buck tag was filled. He was a six-point, weighing around 130 pounds. I called him my "Halloween buck." Dave came to help me drag my buck to the skinning gantry. Every camp needs a Dave, for sure.

November 2 finally arrived, and hopefully an end to three months of pain. Surgery to remove that finger joint, scheduled for 10:00 AM, was completed. My left hand was sporting a huge bandage. A follow-up appointment took place two weeks later. In the meantime, a big surprise occurred in the presidential election, November 8. Donald Trump won and would be our next president. Dave and I had been remarking about the huge number of Trump signs along the route from Chambersburg to camp, and the almost complete lack of signs supporting Clinton. Still, the results amazed us, given that the media said he had no chance.

The Halloween buck

The bandage on my left hand made it inconvenient for bear hunting, but manageable. The biggest problem with the finger was that it got painfully cold. We hunted from stands on the opening day, Saturday, November 19. No bears were seen. On Sunday, we got together with the Giovannitti camp and planned some drives for the following day. On Monday morning, the group got together at our cabin, and plans were finalized. I decided to participate in some of the drives. The first one started on Jersey Hollow Road across from Bob Mitchell's house, ran parallel to Back Road, and ended at Camp Rip-N-Tear. The new knees were working great, and I managed pretty well until I got to the hillside close to camp. I didn't remember it as being so steep, but then, I was cruising up on 75 years of age like a runaway freight train. No bears were moved to our standers on this drive.

The second drive was in the area of Conn Road. Being a stander on this drive, I saw several does and a nice buck go by. On the third drive I was again a driver. This one started at the Steinmiller camp and ended at the swamp just beyond Scott's camp. As before, deer were moved, but no bears. A neighbor, Jim Procyson, showed up at camp that afternoon and reported that he had shooting at a bear in the morning, not too far from where we did our first drive. Maybe we did move one.

We broke bear camp on Tuesday, with our friend, Stan Rice, staying on to hunt one more day. Larry and I both had doctor appointments scheduled for Wednesday, so we had to leave.

Larry had been having problems with his sense of balance. I have to interject a short story here. Larry's problem was diagnosed as a condition called vestibulitis, which is an inflammation of the inner ear. This causes a loss in sense of balance. We first encountered this condition in the early 1980's when Pat Haller's English setter Duchess developed a condition where she seemed prone to falling down. It was diagnosed by Doctor John Fague, a Shippensburg veterinarian, as vestibulitis. He called it "old rolling dog syndrome." Duchess survived it, so when one of our setters developed it, we knew it was not fatal. I joked with Larry about being part dog, and referred to him as the old rolling dog.

As is traditional in Pennsylvania, rifle deer season began Monday after Thanksgiving. Dave and I arrived in camp on Saturday. We spent the two days scouting for deer, enjoying my cooking, and watching football on TV. Larry arrived Sunday afternoon. The week was interesting, to say the least. We did not notice a lot of hunting pressure in our area. The only hunters in evidence were those from the Steinmiller camp and ours. In order to hunt in our little corner, one has to walk at least a quarter mile off the road just to get to our cabin. We had three hunters in camp for the entire week (Dave, Larry, and yours truly) and were joined at times by Crawford, Dave's nephew Judd, and Stan Rice. The only tag for deer I had left was a DMAP permit for the Mt. Davis area, so I drove the fifteen miles to hunt there the first morning. It had been many years since I encountered so many hunters in the woods on the first day of rifle deer season. Cars and trucks were parked everywhere. After trying to get away from the orange army for a couple of hours, I gave up and went back to camp to cook dinner.

Dave and Larry reported in shortly after dark. Each had seen deer, but the only buck Dave saw was a four-point, which has not been a legal buck since antler restrictions went into effect in 2001. Dinner was the venison tenderloin recipe I stole from a poster named Zummer on the huntingpa website. As usual, there were no leftovers.

Tuesday was another day in the woods for Dave and Larry. I read a David Baldacci novel and did a couple of short pushes for the guys. Stan did a walkabout, covered a lot of ground, and saw plenty of deer. Dave and Larry did mostly stand hunting and saw fewer. Larry had still not seen a buck, but Dave had one of the big boys cruise past his stand at Mach 8. He was unable to get off a shot.

Wednesday I was out and about since bear season had reopened. While there was enough bear sign in the area to get us excited, we did not see any of them. Crawford showed up and saw seven deer, one of which was a legal buck, but Crawford is picky and passed on him. Toward evening, Larry saw a bruiser with what he described as a "wide rack," and got off a shot. No blood was found. We looked for about an hour and a half, so we cut off one more shirt tail for the wall. This is a tradition in hunting camps. If a hunter misses an easy shot, he loses part of his shirt tail.

Larry's Thursday nine-point

Thursday was Larry's day. I know you all will understand when I say that we hunters work hard and hope for something good. It happened for Larry. Wouldn't you know that, while sitting under the same hemlock tree, the same buck came past. Larry downed him with one shot. Shortly after hearing the shot, I received a text message on my cell phone asking me to bring the deer cart. When I got there, he had the buck just about gutted. I took one look at it and said, "I think we need Dave." With a lot of grunting, cussing, and of course, Dave, we managed to get the buck back to camp. The PGC's weight tape estimated the buck at 161 pounds dressed. Outside spread was seventeen inches. Officially it was a nine-point with three fighting tines broken. We knew it was the same buck because it had a crease on its back where Larry's Wednesday shot grazed it.

As is obvious from the broken tines, this buck was a real fighter. In the photograph, between the wheel on the deer cart and Larry's elbow, the crease cut by Larry's shot the day before along the backbone can be seen. We have skinned and butchered a bunch of deer in the decade since we started hunting here. This buck stood out as being different. Two things were unusual about this one. The first was that it had very little fat stored for the winter. Most of the deer we harvest are rolling fat. Second, the hide was much tougher than usual. Dave and I dulled several knives while skinning it. We suspected this would turn out to be tough venison, so our advice to Larry was to get the entire deer ground into hamburger and add a lot of pork. He decided to keep out the tenderloins and try them. It turned out to be the toughest deer meat he had ever tried to chew. This may have been a really old deer.

The rest of the week was uneventful, with the exception of Stan taking a button buck on Saturday when antlerless deer became legal. No bears were sighted, but there was a good amount of sign. We were puzzled as to why we didn't see any. One interesting thing was that we never saw many hunters other than those in our group. I guess this was because one has to walk at least a quarter mile from any road to our camp and then walk some more to get into the good hunting areas. Most hunters are not all that ambitious anymore. Dave saw three other hunters, Larry saw none, Crawford saw none, Stan saw five, and I saw three. We heard more shooting on Saturday than all the other days combined, probably since antlerless deer were legal. Very few of those shots seemed to be close to camp. I doubt that this area ever had a pumpkin patch or orange army. It is just too far out there. I am sure, however, that hunting pressure is a lot less than it was twenty years ago. One thing we did notice was a lot of traffic along Back Road. I guess road hunting is more fun and less work.

I enjoyed my week at camp, even though I had no deer tag to fill. No time spent in camp is wasted. Since we were done hunting, at least until the primitive weapons season after Christmas, we closed and winterized Camp Rip-N-Tear Saturday, December 3.

The next evening, I received a phone call from Ron Steinmiller telling me that his brother Rick had died. I had visited Rick the first week of rifle season at their cabin. He did not look good, but nobody expected this. Rick was only fifty-one years old. That is way too young to die. Rick had his problems in recent years, including a bout with alcoholism which he beat. Actually, he had pretty much recovered from that, but was dealing with a few other problems, including heart blockage. Over the years, we had become the sort of friends where a phone call out of the blue would not be unusual.

Addendum: I sent the following letter to Ron.

December 4, 2016

Ron:

Please accept my condolences on the passing of your brother Rick. There is no way for me to know how hard this must hit you, so I won't even try. Your phone call this evening hit me like a ton of bricks. Rick did not look well when I saw him at his camp on Tuesday, and as I remember, we discussed that one evening this past week. We were both worried about him, and I guess our worries were justified. I hate to be right about such stuff.

We first met Rick when we bought our camp from his uncle Steve back in 2007. After a bit of a rough start, we got along famously, and I considered him a friend, which is saying something since I really don't have all that many of them. He had his troubles, what with going through a divorce, the cabin break-in, and his bout with demon rum, but he tried to maintain a positive attitude. When I bought my 1911 .45 ACP, it was Rick that I went to for instructions as to how to break it down and clean it. We kept in touch via email, and I was never surprised to get a phone call on occasion when he just wanted to chew the fat for a bit. I know he was really proud of how Hank and Chad were turning out.

The Back Road camp scene will not be the same now without Rick. I do hope we continue to see you there from time to time. You are always welcome at Camp Rip-N-Tear, and you don't even have to bring your own beer (L).

Most sincerely,

George Naugle

2017: *Where did the Bears Go?*

As an extension of the previous story. The Year From Hell, we had to put our old dog Henry down on Friday, January 6. His health had been sliding downhill for several years. We will miss him, as we miss all of our furry family members when they depart this life.

Hunting wise, this year began with Dave, Crawford, and me going out to camp for a few days of late flintlock season hunting the first weekend of the new year. Stan Rice showed up on Friday afternoon and told of having seen a herd of about twenty deer in Glade Run Hollow off Scott Camp Road. He did take a shot, but missed. That scattered the herd. Both Dave and Crawford, who were hunting along the western edge of Glade Run Hollow, saw some of them. Neither took shots. As I was hunting another area, I never saw those deer or any others.

Saturday morning, January 7, I took a long walkabout. I started out on the neighboring property along Back Road and worked my way out the hollow to the north of camp until I came to the third food plot, then climbed the hill, emerging on Harbaugh Road close to the oak flat. Along the way I cut NUMEROUS deer tracks in the fresh snow, perhaps thirty or so, all heading uphill. At the edge of the second food plot, it appeared that a herd of about a dozen had crossed into the oak flat. Obviously, more deer survived hunting season than we imagined. The highlight of the day happened near dark while Crawford occupied the rock stand. A group of deer, one of which was a huge buck that had already lost his antlers, ran past him within easy shooting range. He let them pass, again deciding not drop the hammer. We planned to return to camp sometime later in January to remove ladder stands from the game lands, so all of us left early on Sunday morning.

As is usual for us, we make several trips to camp each winter. On these camp visits, we fire up the woodstove, fill the feeder, download photos from the game cameras, and do a walkabout or two to inventory game. During the cold part of the year, sitting on the porch is not a possibility, but we enjoy swapping lies inside where it is warm. There is always firewood to cut, and while we burn a lot of wood during winter and early spring, we manage to get the porch amply supplied by the time trout season rolls around in April. There are plenty of dead trees on our twenty-two acres, so firewood is always available.

I returned to camp frequently in April, and the weather was quite variable. Sometimes it would be fairly nice, but on other occasions it reminded me that camp is in Somerset County. It snowed three inches or so on Friday, April 7, with a morning temperature of 25°. I watched the deer and turkeys come in during the snowstorm. The next morning, a flock of about twenty turkeys, including six gobblers, crossed the sewer line and hung around the cabin for close to an hour. There was lots of gobbling and strutting. Between 7:30 and 8:00, a buck came in. It was obvious that he had already started to grow this year's rack. This is what spring is like at camp. I usually leave winter behind as I exit Somerset County and enter Bedford County on my way home.

Later in the day on Monday, a bear came to visit the feeder. He banged the tray with his paw to get more corn out. That night he tore the top off the feeder, apparently crawled down inside, took the 4 X 4 I had put in to restrict the flow of corn out, and carried it away a short distance. He then cleaned the feeder completely out. We would need to get the hanging feeder back in operation soon if we wanted to continue feeding.

Snow on April 7 (The temperature was 25° at 7:00 AM.)

We did have some gobblers available for spring hunting as evidenced by several photos showing groups of five or more on a number of occasions. At least two of them were really nice, and one had a beard that nearly dragged on the ground as he walked. Several individual hens came in to the feeder alone. I wondered if they had nests established already.

A group of gobblers and hens (The six birds to the right are gobblers.)

Spring gobbler season could best be described as having been a washout. It rained frequently, and no gobbling was heard. I tried calling, but with no positive results. After giving it the old college try for a few weeks, I stopped hunting spring gobblers. If they didn't gobble, I was at a loss as to how to proceed. (It could be that our season beginning the last Saturday in April is scheduled too late, and breeding activity ends by the time we get started hunting. Oh well. There are always trout to catch.)

As previously mentioned, the roof over the back porch bunkroom was still leaking. The only solution appeared to be replacing the shingles with a metal roof. This project was scheduled for the weekend of July 7-9. Dave and I spent a couple of days in preparing for the big project. We tore off the old roof over the open part of the back porch and set rafters so that the guys could put a proper roof over it. (It had nearly collapsed during the huge snow storm in March of 2010. Dave and I installed some temporary bracing, which became nearly permanent from then until this year.) A week later, Crawford and I measured the roof. We made a list of materials and dimensions. I went to KeyState Metals in Somerset and ordered the roofing materials in Ivy Green to match the color of the shed's roofing.

I arrived on Thursday, July 6, to take delivery of the roofing materials which came that afternoon. Crawford brought two of his friends, Matt Clusman and Rob Matthews, to camp early the next day. Crawford's brother-in-law Stan showed up shortly after them.

Starting almost at once, the guys put on the lath boards. I served as ground man. They did the brute work, screwing the boards down to form a base to which the metal roofing would be attached. This process was interrupted by a thunderstorm toward afternoon. Saturday morning, the last of the lath boards were put on, and they began installing the metal roofing, starting with the front porch roof, then proceeding up to the roof peak. Dave arrived Saturday afternoon and put up scaffolding. This made attaching the last sheets of metal and the corner piece much safer and easier. Once again, a thunderstorm interrupted the process late in the afternoon.

On Sunday morning, the last of the roofing was attached. Crawford, Stan, Matt, and Rob departed for home, leaving Dave and me to mop up. Dave also put a coat of paint on the windows (We have been postponing this for some years.) and we took down the scaffolding. On Monday, we sealed around the chimney and vent pipes and finished fastening the corner pieces on the east side. We did this from a ladder. I left for home when we finished. Dave stayed until Tuesday to relax for another day. A few photos of the roofing project follow. It sure does look nice, and it should last for many years.

The lath goes on. Stan climbs the ladder while Matt, Rob, and Crawford attach the lath boards.

The last corner piece is installed. Stan, Matt, and Dave work from the scaffold.

Finally, the roof was finished and the satellite dish reinstalled.

The following weekend, Crawford, Karen, and some friends went to camp, hoping to go kayaking on the Youghiogheny River. However, there was a huge thunderstorm that washed out Jersey Hollow Road and did major damage to some of the cabin driveways, including ours. It also prevented them from kayaking. When they returned home, Crawford sent me a text message telling me that the six-wheeler was (again) "broke." I began thinking about a replacement.

Over the past year, the vision in my left eye had become increasingly cloudy. What vision I now had in that eye seemed similar to looking through a thick fog. Dr. David Warrow, a retina specialist (and miracle worker), performed a minor operation to fix that problem on August 8. Fluid in that eye between the retina and lens (vitreous humor) was removed and replaced by needle with saline solution. Sort of like getting an oil change? The problem is gone, and my vision is clear again.

Three of us visited camp during mid-August. While I recuperated from the eye surgery, Larry and Dave tilled the three food plots (on the sand mound, the one next to the cabin, and the plot in the hollow along Drake Run). They discovered that we had a problem with people on ATVs going in the old logging road along Drake Run and tearing up that food plot. We finally had to install a gate there. It is disgusting how people do not respect what others own. We have very visible "No Trespassing" signs all around our boundary. Our law enforcement officers seemingly consider trespassing to be of minor importance, so we can expect little to no help from them.

As the old six-wheeler had finally bitten the dust, it needed to be replaced. It sat there in front of the shed for over a month. I told the guys several years earlier that if Crawford could make the old machine last a few more years, I would buy a new one. That time had come, so I ordered a Kubota four-wheeler with dump cart, blade, and winch on August 29.

As a coincidence, August 29 was the last date our game camera took a photo of a bear. Since we were used to seeing them much of the time, it was simply amazing to us that they had disappeared. Where did the bears go? As this was another year with a poor acorn crop, perhaps they went where they could find some.

The weekend of September 14-16, Dave and Larry went to camp to finish erecting tree stands. I couldn't make it due to an illness. Dave noted that we had to replace some of the ratcheting tie straps.

I took the new four-wheeler out to camp on Friday, September 22. I used the front blade to smooth out the driveway, but we would need some stone to do the job right. The Kubota four-wheeler works great. I also loaded the old six-wheeler on my dump trailer and took it to Crawford's shop. Camp was ready for the opener of archery season September 30. I thought I was ready, but found later on that I really was not, as will be seen later in this narrative.

Larry and I drove out to camp on Friday, September 29. Hunting was very slow for both of us on Saturday and again on Monday morning. What deer we saw did not give us decent opportunities for shots, which turned out to be fortunate for me.

On Monday, Larry went to the rock stand and did have some action. A doe crossed in front of him, and while he waited for the doe to come into the open so he could shoot, another doe "made" him. She stomped and snorted, so that part of the game was over. Shortly after that, a nice buck with unusually white antlers crossed in front of him at a distance of more than sixty yards. He was following the does and went down into the Glade Run creek bottom. Larry thought it may have been at least an eight-point.

While sitting in the good stand Monday morning, I got bored around noon. I ate my lunch, and then, just for something to do, got out my hunting licenses and started reading. I should have done that back in July when I bought them. It turned out that I was barely legal. I did have an antlerless deer license and tag, but my collection of yellow licenses and tags was not nearly as complete as it should have been. I did have a resident combination hunting and fur-taking license, which should have included an antlered or flintlock tag and both a fall and spring turkey tag, but none of those were present. In addition, I did have a bear license, but no bear tag. Down out of the stand I came, and after a change in clothing, I made a hasty 115-mile trip to the sporting goods store where I had bought them. They fixed it for me. I could return to camp and hunt, this time completely legal.

Tuesday, my CRNP Carey Strong removed two keratoses, one on my back and one on my chest. She didn't like the way they looked and sent in samples to be biopsied. The results of the biopsies showed the spots were not cancerous. Following this, I drove out to camp shortly after taking Ms. Doris to lunch.

When I arrived, Larry had already left with plans to hike to the laurel stand. As is often the case, Larry couldn't locate the laurel stand and ended up nearly a half mile from it near the game lands food plots. Larry does get turned around in the woods fairly often, which can be easy to do. He then sneak hunted his way back to camp. I changed into hunting attire and went to the front stand which we had moved closer to the sand mound. Things got interesting close to 6:00 PM when a doe ran past about ten yards in front of me. This woke me up. A few minutes later, I saw movement in the laurel some thirty yards or so to my left. I got the crossbow ready. When a large doe stepped out, I cut an arrow loose. Unfortunately, it hit a twig I had not seen. The arrow went way over the back of the doe and could not be found. A clean miss. I was not all that upset, as I still had my antlerless tag.

Wednesday evening, I hiked to the laurel stand. Again, close to 6:00 PM, I saw movement some sixty yards below me, and a nice sized doe walked out of the laurel. Too far for an ethical shot, so I never even got into position to shoot. A few minutes later, I saw movement in the laurel to my right. This turned out to be another doe, roughly thirty yards from me. When she emerged from the laurel, I had a thirty-yard shot at her, but decided not to take it.

Thursday morning was totally unproductive. Neither Larry nor I saw any deer. Actually, Larry had not seen any deer since Monday. This is typical of early archery season hunting at camp. Things usually heat up later in the month. Rain arrived sometime around noon. We decided to call it a week and go home.

John Haydt and the author with South Carolina bucks

Mugs was scheduled for a pheasant hunt at Royal United on Wednesday, October 11. The owner, Richard Smith, offered a hunt at a reduced price for fifteen pheasants, which had us excited. Unfortunately, the rains arrived and the hunt had to be postponed.

I travelled south to Deerfield Plantation in South Carolina for some of their southern hospitality and deer hunting the following week. My friend Steve Musser went along. One of the three deer I took on that trip was a nice eight-point. The following photo is of my eight-point and John Haydt's monster, a real buck.

While I was away, Doris finally had to have our horse Cecil put down. Cecil had been with us for over 28 years, and in his later life was more of a pet than a work animal. We now have three horses buried on our property.

After returning home, we finally did the pheasant hunt on Wednesday, October 25. Mugs had a blast doing his ten-year-old puppy act. The final consensus was that Dave, Larry, and I do not shoot all that well. Dave left for camp that afternoon. Larry and I drove out on Sunday, October 29, planning to be there the next two weeks. Dave went home shortly after we arrived, citing things on his honey-do list to accomplish.

Hunting for the week took place in cold and very windy weather. The excitement started on Tuesday morning. While I sat in the driveway stand (the stand from which I took the Halloween Buck the previous year) I saw six deer, all does. I could have taken one, but there was no need to do that yet with three deer already in our freezer.

Garrett Blake, a nice young man who is a junior majoring in engineering at West Virginia University, stopped in and visited for awhile. He will soon to be part of the family that bought Rick Sabo's tract (Nick and Jennifer Liokareas). I showed him the corners bordering our properties. While we were walking out the old logging road in the hollow to the north of camp, we almost stepped on a large garter snake. I wondered why he was still out and about with the temperature hovering close to freezing.

It rained on Wednesday, so we began the day in the two condo stands. I hiked down to the big one in the hollow along the creek and Larry went to the mini condo at the sand mound. After awhile, I got tired of not seeing anything, so I left around 9:00 and climbed uphill along the game lands boundary line. As I neared the top, two smaller bucks crossed in front of me. I had a good broadside shot at one of them, a six-point, but declined to take it. Having plenty of venison in the freezer sure does take the pressure off. Larry saw one doe. Dave arrived mid-morning.

That afternoon, I hunted from Craig's wooden stand. Dave went into the cuttings near the laurel stand and saw one buck at a distance, but he could not tell how good it was. Larry returned to the mini condo and saw no deer. Crawford and his buddy Rick got there mid-afternoon and went for a walk so Crawford could show him where some of our stands were.

During Thursday and Friday, we saw quite a few deer. It got exciting for Dave on Thursday, as he saw a nice eight-point at his stand near the oak flat, but did not get a shot. Crawford killed a big doe while hunting at the front stand. It weighed 139 pounds dressed. He also saw a big buck and another four does. Rick watched a doe feeding on the sand mound.

Friday was another day with some rain, but not an intolerable amount. Crawford saw a nice buck and missed him, although some white hair got shaved off the bottom of his rib cage. At 8:30 AM, we received a text from Dave telling us that he had a six-point down. This was the third buck he has taken from the bear stand in the last four years. The buck's rack sported a twelve-inch spread and no brow tines. It weighed 165 pounds live and 139 pounds dressed, exactly the same as Crawford's doe.

The rut was starting. We put a camera out on the sand mound. While doing that, we found that a buck had destroyed a small hemlock sapling by thrashing it with his antlers. He apparently threw a branch from the sapling out on to the driveway and also made several other rubs. We think the buck that did this was the one we were calling "Mister Crab." (Note the claw-like points at the end of both main beams.)

Mr. Crab, a really nice typical ten-point

The only hunter to see deer on Saturday was Crawford. He observed a buck chasing a doe at some distance from the mini condo that evening. We broke camp on Sunday and went home to attend to our honey-do lists, returning on Tuesday of the next week.

By the second week of November, the rut was in full bore. Bucks were chasing does, and there were plenty of rubs and scrapes appearing. Larry continued to see very few deer. On Thursday, he pulled a muscle in his leg, causing him to end his week early. Crawford hunted with us Wednesday and Thursday. Dave and I hunted through Saturday. I had another chance at a doe just before dark on Thursday evening at the rock stand. She came out of the bottom and crossed the path to my left at ten yards from me. This would have been hard to miss had I taken the shot. I did not see any more deer the rest of the week.

On Friday, Dave and I talked to Scott Hamilton. He told us that our neighbor Gerry Timscik killed a big eleven-point the previous day. Scott told us that the buck had crab claws, so we thought it might be Mr. Crab. He sent me the following photo of it. It had a crab claw at the end of only one antler, so it was not Mr. Crab. Gerry hunts with a longbow and carbon arrows, doing it the old-fashioned way. Congratulations to him. His was a heck of a buck.

Gerry Timscik's eleven-point buck

Later on when I talked to Gerry about it, he told an interesting story. He had been washing dishes when he looked out the window above the sink and saw some deer working their way toward his driveway. He quickly grabbed his bow and arrows and sneaked out of his cabin, taking a position behind a small hemlock tree. When the buck emerged, he had a shot of ten yards or so. I believe that when you are supposed to get lucky, you do. The buck weighed over 200 pounds with entrails removed.

In the two weeks of archery hunting during the rut, I saw twenty-five deer and had easy shots at two small bucks and three does that I did not take. Dave's buck and Crawford's doe were the only two deer taken. We anxiously awaited rifle season with a bunch of tags left to fill, and as usual, high hopes.

We took most of a week off and then gave bear hunting a try. Amazingly, there was still no bear sign, which is very unusual for the Camp Rip-N-Tear area. Again, we found very few acorns, and that is probably why. With no bears in the area, we spent Saturday hunting in the rain and got nothing but wet. Dave supplied our last piece of bear meat from two years ago. I ground it up and made chili. Crawford went home early on Sunday. We had an inch or two of snow on Monday morning, which made visibility super. I saw eight deer, one of them a really big eight-point. Dave stayed until Monday afternoon. Tuesday morning, while hunting in the mini condo, I saw a great seven-point and a doe. The seven-point's rack appeared to be at least eighteen inches wide. The only photo we ever got of him was this one. I had plenty of time to watch him with binoculars.

The seven-point passes the sand mound.

We did get some photos of a monster eight-point. Perhaps the best one was this one. It showed that he probably had a 22 to 24 inch spread.

This is the monster eight-point. From this and other photos,
I estimated his weight at over 200 pounds!

I remained in camp until Wednesday noon since we had an appointment for direct TV to fix our system. The technician installed a new satellite receiver, and the TV is working again. I left for home around 11:00 with snow coming down. In the previous three weeks, my count of deer seen had risen to about three dozen. The next day being Thanksgiving, the annual family dinner took precedence over hunting. Crawford and Karen hosted us with some family help, providing a turkey and all the trimmings. A day of eating and football is our Thanksgiving tradition.

Dave, Larry, Crawford, and I arrived at camp on Sunday. We watched some football, ate the traditional stew, and prepared ourselves for hunting the next day. That first day of rifle season was not one to write home about. Larry did not see a deer. Dave sat on the bear stand most of the morning and also saw none. I tried the front stand for a few hours and saw nothing, so I moved to the rock of ages chair stand at 9:00. This stand is one along the rim of Drake Run Hollow. I take a folding chair there and have a view of much of the creek bottom below. After an hour or so, I had to get up for a call to nature. When I stood up, I saw a tail exiting toward Back Road. There may have been more than one. I have no idea whether it was a buck or doe, only that it was a deer.

Around 1:00, I had a call from Crawford, telling me that Doris was in the emergency room at Chambersburg Hospital. I beat it home and found that while they had suspected a TIA or a mini stroke, the tests they performed were not conclusive. They kept her overnight for observation. On Tuesday morning when she returned home, she decided to walk Mugs. Since she felt well enough to do that and go to her animal shelter board meeting that evening, I returned to camp. Dave called while I was on the way to report that he had seen a number of deer, including three bucks Tuesday morning as he sat in the driveway stand. He moved one ladder stand to a spot in the thick laurel across the driveway from the cabin.

Garrett Blake emailed me some photos of a buck he had taken. He called it Wishbone (note the left antler). He shot it at 8:30 AM on Tuesday. We had photos of this buck at the sand mound, taken earlier in November, and also one of him in June when he was in velvet.

Garrett Blake is happy with Wishbone.

I hunted without success on Wednesday. On Thursday morning, I sat in the mini condo. At 6:50, the seven-point appeared. By 6:55, it became light enough that I could see he was legal, so I ended my buck season. Nobody was in camp when I finished dragging him to the skinning gantry, so I have no proper hero shot. Dave took the following photo with his cell phone of some old guy holding the buck's antlers.

This is a nice set of antlers, but who is this old guy?

During the week, Larry saw very few deer. Dave, who was without a buck tag, saw a bear shortly after 5:00 PM on Wednesday, so he spent the rest of the week hunting where he had seen it. This was our first bear sighting since August. Unfortunately, the bear never reappeared.

On Saturday morning, Larry finally gave up his quest for a rack buck and settled for a young antlerless deer. It turned out to be a button buck. The meat should be much better eating than that from a larger deer anyway. We broke camp and went home that morning after skinning and quartering his deer. On my way home, I delivered the deer carcasses to the Grove butcher shop in Saint Thomas for processing.

Larry with a button buck, our fourth deer taken this season

Crawford and I returned to camp to hunt the last three days of rifle deer season. While he still had not filled his buck tag, I was hunting only does and was not all that anxious to take one. I now had four deer butchered and in the freezer. By this time, the deer have PhDs in hunter avoidance, so they are really elusive. We did not see many, but we did see enough to keep us interested.

Friday evening while sitting at the rock stand, I stuck it out until very close to dark. When I finally decided I had enough, I stood up to get my gear together. Wouldn't you know it? Two deer had sneaked in from the creek below. When they saw me, they ran back where they came from. The same evening, Crawford saw a buck at the laurel stand but did not have a decent shot.

Late Saturday afternoon, I had three does come out of the woods close to the blowdown stand. While I could easily have killed any one of the three, I decided not to do so. Taking one of the easy shots would have necessitated dragging a deer to the cabin and then skinning it in the dark before supper. It was not a tough decision, considering that I already had a freezer full of venison.

Sunday morning, Crawford and I put up the trash can feeder and winterized the cabin. We planned to return to camp after Christmas and do some flintlock or archery hunting, but this ended our hunting year. Another great year, 2017, goes into the books. As someone once said, hunting sure beats working, doesn't it?

The saga of my hunting camps does not end here. After all, another hunting season is just around the corner, and I am already looking forward to it. This will continue until I stop getting excited about a coming hunting season or I finally decide I am too old to hunt anymore. It may end when I depart this mortal coil. Actually, it will continue as long as someone in the family thinks hunting camp is a great place to be, and I am on the green side of the grass. I hope the reader has enjoyed my ramblings about these two special places in my heart. I also hope this makes some think about having such camps for themselves. As a good friend used to say, "You done the easy part. You talked about it."

Log of game taken at Camp Rip-N-Tear

2007: George-October 8-doe with crossbow (first camp kill)
Crawford-November 30- doe

2008: Crawford-turkey (first fall turkey)
George-doe
Dave-doe
Larry-8-point buck (first buck for the camp) and doe the same day
Nick-doe rifle

2009: Dave-doe in early muzzleloader season
George-6-point buck (170 lbs.)
George, Dave, and Nick- does

2010: George-8-point buck (135 lbs.)
Dave-5-point buck

2011: Crawford-spring gobbler
Stan-two spring gobblers (first spring gobbler)
Larry and George- does
Dave-8-point buck(140 lbs.)
Georg–8-point buck (165 lbs.)

2012: Larry-doe and beautiful 8-point buck (150 lbs. buck)
Dave-doe and 7-point buck
George-bear (first bear kill for camp)
George-button buck

2013: Dave-doe (174 lbs)
Seth-doe (140 lbs)
George-5-point buck (120 lbs.)
George-DMAP doe from Mt. Davis (our first kill on the big mountain).

2014: Dave-doe and buck (4 points on one side, antler broken on other side)
Seth-doe
George-doe

2015: George-spring gobbler
Dave-buck(4 points on one side, long spike on other – 150 lbs)
George-9-point buck (17 inch spread – 184 lbs)
George-bear (taken on a drive with Giovannitti camp)
Larry-buck (4points on one side, antler broken on other – 139 lbs.)

2016: George-doe
George-6-point buck (130 lbs)
Larry-9-point buck (17 inch spread – 161 lbs)
Stan Rice- button buck

2017: Crawford – doe
Dave-6-point buck
George-7-point buck (17 inch spread)
Larry-button buck

Totals:
does – 21
bucks – 17
turkeys – 5
bears – 2